Michael Oakeshott as a Philosopher of the "Creative"

And Other Essays

Wendell John Coats Jr.

imprint-academic.com

Published in the UK by
Imprint Academic, PO Box 200, Exeter EX5 5YX, UK

Distributed in the USA by
Ingram Book Company,
One Ingram Blvd., La Vergne, TN 37086, USA

ISBN 9781845409937 Hardback

A CIP catalogue record for this book is available from the
British Library and US Library of Congress

To the memory of Michael J. Oakeshott (1901–1989), exquisite cultivator of the complex Western urge to stand both within and without the stream of time, to appreciate the unique historical event, and yet to rise above it…

And to the memory as well of Michael B. Foster (1903–1959), profound expositor of the distinction between a crafted object and a created object (to include a human being), and the various philosophic and cultural ramifications thereof…

Contents

Preface

Thanks to the Michael Oakeshott Association at the conferences of which many of these papers were first presented; to Imprint Academic for permission to reprint the first and seventh essays;[1] to Lexington Books for permission to reprint the third essay;[2] to Associated University Presses for permission to reprint the fourth essay;[3] to the Association for Core Texts and Curricula for permission to reprint as an appendix my little talk on medieval 'Eternity-Creation' debates;[4] to Bodleian Library, Oxford University, for providing a copy of the Liddington thesis; and to Connecticut College for a semester sabbatical leave in 2018 to write the fifth and sixth essays. Thanks also to Sharon Moody for daring, yet again, to type from my tortured scrawl; and to Tim Fuller, Bob Grant, Pamela Jensen, Sylvia Lechner, and Noel O'Sullivan for comments on various essays. Obviously I alone am responsible for not taking more of their advice than I did.

1   "Michael Oakeshott as Philosopher of 'the Creative'", in O'Sullivan, N. (ed.) (2017) *The Place of Michael Oakeshott in Contemporary Western and Non-Western Thought*, pp. 123–141; "Politics, the Political and Armed Force", in *Collingwood and British Idealism Studies*, Vol. 22, No. 2, 2016, pp. 257–277.

2   "Some Correspondences between Michael Oakeshott's Critique of Rationalism and A.C. Graham's Account of 'Spontaneity' vs. Reason'", in Coats Jr., W.J. & Cheung, C.-Y. (2012) *The Poetic Character of Human Activity*, pp. 41–55, Lanham, MD: Lexington Books.

3   "Oakeshott's Descartes, Vico's Descartes", in Coats Jr., W.J. (2003) *Political Theory and Practice*, pp. 43–57, London: Associated University Presses.

4   "Modern Political Effects of Medieval 'Creation–Eternity Debates'", in *Proceedings of 2014 ACTC Conference*, online publication, coretexts.org.

Introduction

These eight essays of mine, with one exception, were all written within the past few years. They explore and elucidate *aspects* of the thought of the twentieth-century English philosophic essayist, Michael Oakeshott, *some* of which have not been addressed in contemporary secondary literature on his work. As is often observed, Oakeshott's was an original and enigmatic mind which it is difficult to categorize — conservative, classical liberal, post-modernist, philosophic Idealist, philosophic skeptic, etc. (?) Nor, in the case of Oakeshott, is there much profit to be had in that kind of categorizing exercise. Readers are invited to follow for their own sake Oakeshott's insightful observations on a variety of subjects, as explored in these collected essays, which advance the view that *much* of Oakeshott's work can be seen as a tale spun around the central insight that the structure of experiential reality is creative or poetic.

The title essay, "Michael Oakeshott as a Philosopher of the 'Creative'", is my attempt, after several decades of reflection and writing on his work,[1] to provide a comprehensive view of Oakeshott's perspective on the human things, including, saliently, political life. The essay attempts to place Oakeshott within a narrative of Western intellectual life viewed as embodying a *tension between* the Greek rationalist philosophy of Plato and Aristotle, *and* biblical (Jewish and Christian) wilful, creation accounts. Oakeshott is seen as siding increasingly, as he matured, with the "creative" side of the tension. The essay also advances the argument that what Oakeshott called "the poetic character of human activity" is not merely an expression of a preference for an aesthetic view of life, but rather an ontological claim that the structure of experiential reality itself is "creative" or "poetic", with the form (*how*) and content (*what*) of experience and activity arising simultaneously and conditioning one another reciprocally; and

---

[1] This includes two (one co-authored) previous collections of essays on Oakeshott, and a 1985 journal article on his work which Oakeshott wrote to me and others that he liked.

that this claim has profound philosophic, political, moral, and policy effects.

The next four essays hang together thematically. The *second* essay explores the theme of the "creative" from the standpoint of "modernity" and "post-modernity". The *third* essay attempts to show the correspondences between Oakeshott's critique of prosaic Rationalism and the ancient Chinese Daoist critique (expounded by A.C. Graham) of Confucian and Mohist rationalism. The *fourth* essay explores Oakeshott's critique of Modern Rationalism by way of comparison *of* his abbreviated critique of Cartesian philosophy *and* that of the eighteenth-century professor of rhetoric, G.B. Vico. The *fifth* essay contrasts the views of Oakeshott and Leo Strauss on the ancient Romans and Roman law in the history of Western political thought and practice. Predictably, Oakeshott is more appreciative of the Roman emphasis on unreflective and creative tradition *versus* the Greek orientation on rational "blueprint". The essay also inspects Oakeshott's criticism of the misguided attempt to conflate the Greek and Roman experiences, *à la* Strauss. The *sixth* essay replies to an acute and critical analysis by John Liddington of Oakeshott's account of *both* experience *and* civil association and the state, by arguing that Oakeshott's coherence theory of truth comprehends the correspondence theory, and not the other way around as Liddington would have it.

The last two essays are not expressly linked to the theme of the "creative" but are of compelling interest in their own right. The *seventh* summarizes the views of Oakeshott and the twentieth-century philosopher of science, A.N. Whitehead, on education and observes how the latter's more utilitarian defence of learning for its own sake supports Oakeshott's views. The *eighth* essay compares Oakeshott's view on the relationship *of* armed force and war to *politics* with that of the German thinkers Carl Schmitt and Max Weber, and argues that Oakeshott's view is closer to Aristotle's in declining to view politics as simply another form of the will to power.

Although these essays address some scholarly issues (especially in the footnotes), they should be of interest to generally educated readers versed in the perennial themes of higher human reflection. In an attempt to convey quickly the importance of the theme of the "creative" in both philosophy and practical life, included as an appendix is a little talk I gave on modern political effects of medieval "creation-eternity" debates. The sixth essay is the only one addressed exclusively to Oakeshott scholars and scholars of British and German philosophic Idealism.

One

Michael Oakeshott as a Philosopher of the "Creative"

"...the characteristic developments of modern political theory have depended on the displacement of the concept of information by that of creation as the highest practical activity... the same displacement has influenced the modern concept of artistic activity." —M.B. Foster, 1935.

This paper advances the argument that the work of the twentieth-century political philosopher, Michael Oakeshott, may be coherently viewed as an increasingly explicit appreciation of what I am calling "the creative" in human thought and action, and what Oakeshott himself alluded to as "the poetic character of human activity". I have advanced this thesis for many years, but never attempted a comprehensive statement of it showing both its meaning across Oakeshott's various works, as well as how it fits in the context of Western philosophy from Plato to the twenty-first century. Thus, this paper is an attempt to show not only the presence of a unifying theme across Oakeshott's various works beginning with *Experience and Its Modes* (1933), but also how this theme fits in and helps to elucidate and advance the various philosophic and political themes of Western modernity and post-modernity. In brief, and to get ahead of ourselves, I shall be trying to show that the general drift and outline of Western philosophy and political philosophy can be manageably perceived from the late medieval period onward as an increasingly explicit argument *between* the cosmological, ontological, and ethical assumptions of ancient Greek rationalism *and* the implied assumptions of the Judaic and Christian biblical inheritance over the issue of "the creative" in cosmology, history, and conduct, to the increasing favour by late modernity of the latter, whether explicitly so or not; and that Oakeshott's is an important twentieth-century voice echoing for the most part in and within the tones and perspective of "the creative" *versus* the Greek rationalist side of the debate.

The case for this argument will be laid out in stages. The first will be to contrast the differences *between* (1) the Greek rationalist (especially Platonic) view of the eternity of the universe, and its implications for politics and ethics, *and* (2) the biblical (especially Maimonidian) view of the creation of the universe and its implications for ethics and politics. The second stage will be to show how the conception of the creative in human experience appears in Oakeshott's writing with increasing explicitness in *and after* the essays of the 1940s and 1950s collected in *Rationalism in Politics*. The third stage of the argument will be to show how Oakeshott's understanding of the poetic or creative character of human thought and activity compares and contrasts with the views of other twentieth-century thinkers such as Charles Taylor, Fredrich Hayek, Alasdair MacIntyre, and Leo Strauss.

I. "The Creative"

Since the aim of this paper is to fit Oakeshott's work into a "meta-narrative" about the tensions *between* the Greek rationalist and biblical inheritances of Western civilization, it will be necessary to reach back and summarily indicate the salient issues here. At stake here will be the answers to three broad questions: (1) what kind(s) of activities may be done for their own sake; (2) are there any antecedently existing ideas, or is intellect always and inextricably entwined with previous experience and action; and (3) given the answers to these questions, what is the basis for sound and skilful human moral and political practice.

Let us begin by summarily contrasting the Greek and biblical inheritances on these kinds of questions by focusing on the difference *between* a created *and* an eternal, teleologically purposive universe; and *between* a created *and* a crafted object (to include a human being). The best place to start is with the Jewish philosopher Moses Maimonides' twelfth-century Arabic language masterpiece, *The Guide of the Perplexed*. (Maimonides is better suited for our purposes than Aquinas in the *Summa Theologica* who is generally concerned to minimize the differences between the Greek and biblical inheritances in order to synthesize them.) Maimonides is explicit about the way in which the biblical account of wilful creation *ex nihilo* denies the possibility of an eternal, teleological universe ordered toward a final end, as in the Greek rationalist accounts. On the biblical account of the universe ("the All"), the only thing which can be said of God's creation is that it is God's volition and is created "for no other purpose" than God's glory:

> Thus… the quest for a final end of all collapses. For we say that in virtue
> of this will He has brought into existence all of the parts of the world,
> some of which have been intended for their own sakes. (Maimonides,
> 1963, p. 452)

And Maimonides also distinguishes the biblical account of creation *ex
nihilo* from the Platonic account of a divine craftsman in *The Timaeus*
who moulds or crafts pre-existing matter into pre-existing forms – the
believer in the Law of Moses and Abraham "is to believe that there is
nothing eternal in any way… with God", and that "the bringing into
existence out of non-existence is for the deity not an impossibility…"
(*ibid.*, p. 285).

Let us draw out more fully the (implied) differences between the
Greek rationalist and the biblical accounts in this connection. As is
generally known, on the Greek rationalist worldview, both form and
matter are given eternally; the essence of any object is its "detachable"
form; matter adds nothing positive to form; and both thinking and
making are purposive and involve discovering and copying pre-
existing forms or models. By contrast, as we have just noted in
Maimonides' text, the account of cosmological creation in the sacred
Hebrew and Christian texts entails the ideas that creation is not
purposive in the Greek sense, that is, it is not directed toward a
distinctively conceived and antecedently existing form or end in
advance of the act of wilful creation; and, by implication, in creation,
and in a created (versus a crafted) object there is no intellectively
graspable form distinguishable from its accidental embodiment.

Several more implications follow. Creation is an act of will which
can exceed regulations prescribed by reason. Contingency is an important aspect of created objects (including physical nature and human
beings), that is, their "accidental" embodiments are not necessitated by,
nor can be deduced from, their form or idea. And, finally, there can be
no degrees of being in creation as there are in the Greek idea of substance (*ousia*): if something is created *ex nihilo*, "it must be entirely
present as soon as it has ceased to be wholly absent" (Foster, 1934, p.
464).

To continue this accelerated narrative, Maimonides' account of
divine, creative will is taken to an extreme in the thought of the late
medieval British voluntarist thinkers, Duns Scotus and William of
Ockham, in which both divine and human will become pure,
unlimited, indeterminate power without finality (distinguished from
the older views of both Aristotle and Augustine that human willing is
naturally directed toward what is good). In the words of the contemporary Swiss medieval scholar, Andre de Muralt, with reference to
Scotus and Ockham, "it is between 1250 and 1350… that the premise of

the contemporary intellectual situation appears as well as the decline of a unified philosophic conception of possible human knowledge..." (deMuralt, 1991, p. 39, my translation). And in the case of Ockham, the voluntarist claim is partnered with the nominalist claim that universals are not real but are merely names: *universalia sunt nomina*. This single sentence arguably killed the work of five hundred years of scholasticism as the view spread that there are meanings and representations in the mind but only things in the world, displacing the Aristolian idea that the "beings of the world" were in the soul.

Additionally, in the thought of Ockham, the seeds are sown of the modern Liberal view of liberty as the freedom to act short of harm to another, and of governmental authority as merely an external limit to infinite, individual freedom. Over time, the idea of the infinite freedom of human will (based on a claim of its univocity with divine will) arguably issues in "creative" political alternatives to the Platonic *techne* model of political rule, in which rulers form inert citizen subject matter into pre-existing political forms, as exemplified in great detail in *The Republic*. These alternatives became clearer in the work of Hobbes and Rousseau. In the case of Hobbes, human art imitates divine art (nature) in wilfully constructing the great *Leviathan*; in the case of Rousseau, in direct opposition to Plato and the *techne* model of rule, a sovereign people create, or give themselves, their own political or constitutional forms. In Rousseau's surface vision, people cease to be inert, passive subject matter formed by rulers, and creatively generate and impose upon themselves their own political forms (albeit while being secretly manipulated by philosophy and religion).

The idea of the autonomy of the human spirit will follow Ockham to Germany where he emigrated, and appears in its present form there centuries later in Kantian ethics and its ascription of categorical duties toward others, transcending any claims of the empirical ego; and also in the thought of Hegel who argues that the human spirit can override all antecedent and genetic inheritance. However, it is in the nineteenth-century German neo-Kantian explorations of the disintegrations of the medieval synthesis (in the increasing differentiation and fragmentation of knowledge) that we can see the long-term effects of the spread of the medieval voluntarist conception of the creative will. For it is this conception of a created and contingent reality the implications of which we saw identified by Maimonides, which makes impossible a teleological conception of the world and of nature since all sorts of so-called "lower" beings and purposes are now equally *real*, and not simply diluted forms of reason and intellect, as in the Greek rationalist view. This viewpoint about the reality of matter and the contingency of physical nature not only makes possible modern empirical science, but also modern epistemological and ethical pluralisms, since all sorts of mundane activities can now be done (*contra* Aristotle) for their own sake, and all sorts of knowledge claims can be made for their own sake.

To unpack this idea briefly, it involves a transformation and broadening of the Aristotelian idea of activity done for its own sake. For the ontological dualist, Aristotle, the only activity which can be done purely for its own sake is thought thinking thought, an activity of the Unmoved Mover which thinks itself, and which can be approximated by human beings in philosophic contemplation. And even though Aristotle is more appreciative of the reality of material and practical life than his teacher, Plato, in the end for him matter is still a diminution of Being understood as pure thought. Now, for historically complex reasons involving biblical ideas such as creation and incarnation and sacred history read and discussed in the light of Greek logic, the idea slowly evolved that activities other than *Theoria* could be done and enjoyed for their own sake, owing to the reality of the material and mundane world which in the Christian (especially Augustinian) worldview becomes not a diminution of Being, but an arena for spiritual engagement and growth. One of the first and clearest instances of the view that mundane activity could be done for its own sake and enjoyment (and not simply as a diversion as in the ancient Epicurean view) is to be found in the three volumes of Montaigne's *Essays*. As is well known, at the age of thirty-eight Montaigne retired to his estate and his study in order to construct a private life where he could avoid instrumental purposes as much as practically possible, and engage in various mundane activities such as conversation and friendship for their own sake and enjoyment. And where this was not realistically possible owing to practical obligations, Montaigne preferred to focus on the ritualistic aspects of activity and relationships, since these are more easily thought of as existing for their own sake even where they issue in some practical benefit. (One waits one's turn to speak not merely for the order it produces, but because it is the polite or civil thing to do.) By implication, Montaigne clearly sees himself as a unique, (created) individual in whom "essence" and "accident" cannot be meaningfully separated, as in the ontologically dualist, Greek rationalist account, an individual for whom the most important thing in life is to learn how to belong to himself and cultivate his own ruling form (*forme maitresse*).

Montaigne's cultivation of the diversity and plurality of life for its own sake becomes an epistemological and ontological issue in German philosophy of the nineteenth and early twentieth centuries, especially in neo-Kantianism, where the phenomenon of the radical plurality of modernity is recognized as a problem to be analysed for the difficulties it creates for any unified theory of knowledge and experience. Heinrich

Rickert, for example, in *Kant as Philosopher of the Modern Age* argued that the relative autonomy of thinking, willing, and feeling in Kant's three critiques made him *the* philosopher of a modernity characterized by the claims of each of the three to exist for its own sake, although Rickert himself called for a unified theory of knowledge which could preserve the "many-sidedness" (*Vielseitigkeit*) of reality (Rickert, 1924, p. 150). And in the same generation the highly original thinker, George Simmel, expounded an "aesthetic" view of modernity as historically transcending the more primitive purposive orientation of the teleological or pragmatic human stage in the achieved capacity to pursue various forms or modulations of the whole of experience (such as art, science, and practice) for their own sake (Podoksik, 2015), in an almost ritualistic sense reminiscent of Montaigne's approach to appropriate and contented living. And what is now known as post-modernism, in all its varieties, might be summarily characterized as the attempt at "validation" of all "difference" and particularity, through "deconstruction" of the inherited philosophic, scientific, and political forms of modernity, at whatever cost to structures of authority and stability.

Now, before moving on to an attempt at placing Oakeshott's work in the context of this narrative of the fortunes of the "creative" in Western philosophy and political thought, let us briefly rehearse its themes. Western philosophy is not just a footnote to Plato, because since at least the second century before Christ, Greek philosophy has been in a dialogue with Hebraic creation doctrines; and since the second century after Christ, with Christian creation and incarnation doctrines,[1] i.e. with ideas that the cosmos and the world are not eternal; that divine creative will can create in advance of positing intellective forms and purposes; and that the divine *logos* could somehow be amplified, rather than diminished, through material incarnation. In philosophic terms, this would be to say that the material world is no less real than the intellective world, and hence to deny the possibility of an ascending chain of teleological purposes culminating in a final cause. As we have seen, in a created world and in created objects (including human beings) intellective essence cannot be separated from material "accident" and used as standard by which to judge various historical instantiations. Summarily speaking, in a created (versus an eternal, teleological) universe, contingency will be essential to the idea of physical nature; creativity will be essential in accounting for human thinking and acting, which will not be seen as purposive in the Greek sense of copying distinctively conceived and antecedently existing intellective models; and, by implication, positivity (versus mere

---

1   For more on this, see Dihle (1982).

rationality) will be essential to the idea of law. I have been suggesting that it has been the tension between these two inheritances — the Greek and the biblical, the "intellectual" and the "creative" — which has characterized Western philosophy and science for roughly the past two millennia, and that since about the thirteenth century it has been the "creative" account which has increasingly gained dominance, or at least alternating dominance , over teleological modes of thinking (Thomism and eighteenth-century Enlightenment rationalism to the contrary notwithstanding).

This paper will now attempt to place Oakeshott's work in the context of this compact narrative, but, before doing so, it is important to note that it is possible to come to some of the insights about the creative fluidity of reality and about human skill and moral balance in this light, from non-Western sources, in particular, from classical Chinese Daoist thought (in its contentions with Confucian rationalism), a source which we shall see Oakeshott drew upon in formulating his critique of rationalism in morals and politics.[2]

II. Oakeshott as Philosopher of the Creative

In order to proceed with an investigation for contemporary readers of the theme of the creative or poetic character of human activity throughout Oakeshott's work, it is first necessary to address and declare a position on a major issue in Oakeshott scholarship. This is the question of whether Oakeshott after the 1950s *abandoned* the philosophic Idealism of *Experience and Its Modes* (1933), and its conception of philosophy as experience without arrest on pre-supposition, continually *en voyage* to the ultimate satisfaction of full coherence, for (1) either a Hobbesian-like nominalism; or (2) a modified form of Personal Idealism asserting the primacy of the finite or practical individual; or (3) a sort of neo-Kantian embrace of the modern and postmodern 'fragmentation' of a unified knowledge of any kind.[3] My own view, and the assumption of the analysis which follows, is that there is no compelling reason to assume that Oakeshott did change his fundamental orientation in *Experience and Its Modes*, although his emphasis often changed depending on the subject being investigated, and/or rhetorical considerations vis-à-vis potential readerships. Even the 1958 essay on the voice of poetry and its orientation of image-making within the "conversation of mankind" can be read as metaphorical or even as a view of the whole from a poetic perspective, distinguished from the

---

2   For more on this see Coats and Cheung (2012).
3   For the first view, see Bhuta (2015); for the second, see Podoksik (2012); for a refutation of the third, see Boucher (2012).

focus of *Experience and Its Modes* on the progression of thought itself. The only clear change in his thought after the 1958 essay (which Oakeshott himself obliquely acknowledge) is the recognition of aesthetic experience as a distinct modality or arrested view of the whole of experience itself. And even these who think Oakeshott did abandon Absolute Idealism can hopefully profit from the following investigation which provides a way of looking at the developmental issue in Oakeshott scholarship, from the standpoint of the increasing prevalence of the "creative" in Oakeshott's thought over time. In different words, I will be suggesting that the unifying perspective in Oakeshott's entire *corpus* is arguably the poetic or creative structure of experiential reality; and that the "developmental" change in Oakeshott's view of aesthetic experience may have come from the increasing realization that his own account of the evolution and structure the various modalities of experience was dependent on the "creative" idea that the form and content of experience arise simultaneously and fluidly, and that there are no ascertainable degrees of reality in various determinate modulations of the experience as in a teleological worldview.

With that as a point of departure then, let us take up several salient ways in which Oakeshott's work (increasingly) reflects the insight that the structure of human experience is creative. *First* to consider is the "creative" way in which the various modalities of experience (science, history, practice, art) arise and exist for Oakeshott. *Next* how Oakeshott uses this insight to criticize rationalism in morals and politics. *Next* how Oakeshott's conception of civil association (vs. enterprise association) better accommodates the creative or poetic structure of reality. And, finally, how the theoretical perspective Oakeshott calls "theorizing contingency" reflects the medieval theological insight that in a created being content is not accidental to form, by providing a theoretical perspective capable of explaining an event in human conduct "without explaining it away".

I would like to suggest that Oakeshott's 1933 account of experience and its modalities is a "creativist" account in two important ways — the relationship between and among modalities of experience, and the way in which determinate modalities arise in human experience. As is now generally known, for Oakeshott in *Experience and Its Modes* the drive of human consciousness and experience is toward complete coherence (even if never achieved) and various "modalities" of experience such as "science" and "history" are seen as incomplete assertions, of the whole of reality based upon some mediating principle such as "quantity" or "contiguity". What distinguished Oakeshott's account from those of other Idealist thinkers such as Hegel and Bosanquet and Collingwood was his view that there could be no teleological-like ascending chain of modes of experience distinguished by their increasing logical coherence. Although perhaps a logical possibility, human intellect was not up to the task of establishing or demonstrating this, Oakeshott thought, and, moreover, focusing on this problem directed attention away from the more important idea that each mode of arrest in experience was an assertion about the whole of reality, rather than simply non-entity, and formally equal to other such modes in this respect.

Now, it is here that we can see in Oakeshott's account the similarity and perhaps influence of the medieval voluntarist, "creationist" cosmological account (vs. the rationalist, teleological account). As we saw in the paper's first section, in a created universe, there are no degrees of being as there are in the Greek concept of *ousia*—"if something is created *ex nihilo*, it must be entirely present as soon as it has ceased to be wholly absent" (Foster, 1934, p. 464). Now, this implied the reality of matter (as well as thought) a point which the Idealist Oakeshott would not unqualifiedly admit. Yet, in fact, he approximates this insight in asserting that each modality of experience (such as science) is an assertion about the whole of experience or reality. Since science for Oakeshott mediates experience upon the principle of quantity, and since matter is especially susceptible to conceptualization through quantity, and since human intellect is not up to the demonstrating degrees of failed assertions of reality, assertions about the reality of quantifiable matter must at least be taken as formally equal to the claims of other determinate modes of experience such as those of history and practice. And even philosophy, the unachievable pursuit of full coherence cannot, on Oakshott's account, take the place of arrest or failed attempts in the pursuit of coherence. The implication is that Oakeshott's account of the human experience is structured in such a way as to confirm an important insight from "creationist" theological accounts—reality is not teleologically ordered, and that various assertions of reality must be taken upon their own terms, rather than as diminutions of Being or pure thought as in the Greek rationalist inheritance.

Another way in which Oakeshott's account of experience reflects the creative structure of experiential reality is the way in which determinate modalities arise even though all experience for Oakeshott is viewed as conceptual, with even sense experience simply an incipient form of judgment. For Oakeshott, the form and content (not matter) of experience arise fluidly and spontaneously in tension with one another, with neither more important in creating the modal identity. The formal aspect is the mediating principle (e.g. quantity) and the content is an unidentifiable something until given conceptual identity by the mediating principle. (As Oakeshott would later put it in an essay on teaching and learning, activity arises in a tension between a *how* and *what* of experience, between its form and content.) This is why the logical error of irrelevance (*ignoratio elenchi*) is salient with Oakeshott. That is, various modalities of experience (or later voices in the conversation of mankind) cannot address one another directly because they have no common subject matter to discuss—each determinate modality of experience *creates* its own distinctive subject matter in the way it mediates experience. A scientist, for example, does not study a falling apple, but first resolves it into an abstraction with universal properties called "mass". Or, a historian studies a new subject matter called the historical past, not a common-sensical practical past. And so on. And individual conceptual identities within determinate modes of experience arise in the same "creative" way, not as antecendently existed forms or models to be copied, as in the Platonic *techne* model.

It is this view of the creative structure of experiential reality (what Oakeshott later calls the "poetic character of human activity") which provides the basis for Oakeshott's critique of rationalism in morals and politics in the essays of the 1950s and 1960s. The "blindness" of rationalism (ancient, medieval, and modern) is precisely its failure to perceive the "poetic character" of human activity, that is, the insight that the form and content of all activity, *how* we think or do something and *what* we think or do, arise simultaneously, and condition one another reciprocally, distinguished from the rationalist view that the mind can grasp intellectively antecedently existing forms or models and then prosaically copy them in thought and action. In failing to appreciate the "fluidity" of the relationship *between* moral and political ideals *and* action, rationalism overestimates the capacity of conscious thought to control, and *elevates* what should properly provide a critical faculty in times of moral and political crises and disruption, *into* the source of action itself. In failing to appreciate that it is part of a "process" that reciprocally influences it, rationalism corrodes the moral balance and political skill which grow when the spring of action is largely unreflective. It also corrodes political and other skills when it irrelevently attempts to apply models derived in one activity or sphere of knowledge to another in the mistaken belief that they have a common subject matter.

This insight is a version of the medieval insight that in a created universe (and object, including a human being) the essence and existence of something are of equal importance, neither able to claim ontological priority. Yet, in Oakeshott's thought, there is an additional source for this insight in the classical Chinese Daoist critique of Confucian rationalism, especially in the composite work Oakeshott knew as *Chuang-tzu*. This is the insight that both practical skill and moral balance depend not on "rationally" applying antecedently formulated codes and models, but by acting appropriately and spontaneously in a particular context, and employing analytic intellect only as the protective critic, not instigator, of action. The problem with the former "rationalist" approach, says Oakeshott, is that "self-consciousness is asked to be creative" and "its rule is misrule" (Oakeshott, 1962, p. 75). The rationalist approach to both practical skill and moral balance Oakeshott calls a denial of "the poetic character of human activity". We may also observe that the Doaist account of skill and appropriate thought and action is in accord with Oakeshott's account of the way the form and content of particular modalities of experience evolve fluidly and reciprocally, with neither more important than the other.

Let us now consider my claim that Oakeshott's conception of civil (versus enterprise) association better accommodates what he calls the poetic character of human activity. The reason is, quite simply, that since civil association imposes no unifying, substantive purpose upon a society, it leaves free a realm of activity in which diverse activities can arise spontaneously and "creatively", and in which governmental policy can pursue small, slow changes in accord with a society's "intimations". This is also Oakeshott's defence of institutions of private property and market-economics—civil association, rule of law, and dispersed economic arrangements all nurture the latitude for "creative" responses to the ordeal of consciousness, and, hence, also nurture cultivation of practical skill and moral balance in a society, as well as habits of peace. (For Oakeshott, enterprise association and collectivism arise in conditions of war and tend to perpetuate it.)

Finally, let us consider Oakeshott's account of "theorizing contingency" *as a* reflection of the medieval insight that in a created being content is not accidental to form, and *as a* theoretical perspective capable of explaining an event in human conduct without "explaining it away". In *On Human Conduct* Oakeshott articulates a theoretical perspective which makes explicit an evolved Western understanding of the human ordeal, in which individual actions and utterances are understood as intelligent (or not so intelligent) responses to understood (or misunderstood) situations, distinguished from explanation and understanding in terms of teleological, nomological, and causative processes. Within this realm of *meaning* called "human conduct" Oakeshott also articulates a theoretical perspective capable of explaining particular, individual events without "explaining them away" as they are when explained as effects of teleological processes or as examples of causative processes. Events in the context of "human conduct" are seen as contingently related, that is related and given meaning and intelligibility by being understood *historically*, that is, understood as "touching", or related in being understood responses to similar antecedent events, rather than as examples of some sort of qualitatively different covering law, or teleological process, or organic process. This extraordinarily refined theoretical perspective articulates a view of writing history as the telling of a story with no external meaning, in which events in human conduct are given a conditional intelligibility by being shown to be understood responses to what came before. And I am suggesting that Oakeshott's account of writing history or "theorizing contingency" is a most refined culmination of the medieval insight that contingency is an unavoidable component of a created universe, where contingency is understood to mean that the particulars are not "accidents" of form, nor can be deduced from antecedently existing forms, but arise co-evally with form, and hence can only be accounted for *historically* in human conduct.

III. Oakeshott and Some Contemporaries

The aim of this section is to illustrate the tensions between the rationalist and creativist inheritances and how Oakshott fits in here, by comparing and contrasting his thought with four other twentieth-century thinkers — Charles Taylor, Friedrich Hayek, Alasdair MacIntyre, and Leo Strauss. We shall see that Oakeshott has more in common in this connection with Taylor and Hayek, less with MacIntyre, and least with Leo Strauss, who fixes on the spread of the idea of the "creative" (the extension of the theoretical into the mutable and material) as the source of "modern darkness".

Oakeshott and Charles Taylor share an Hegelian occupation in finding and accounting for the place of the subjective in human experience and history, but in the end Oakeshott is simple less Hegelian and rationalist than Taylor. What does this mean? Arguably, Hegel incorporates in his thought a secularized version of the Christian Trinity and the Incarnation, but not the Hebraic theme of creation, and its implication that will is essential in human action, contingency in nature, and positivity in law.[4] In different words, Hegel remains strongly on the side of the Greek rationalist inheritance on the importance of Reason in human experience except possibly for his historical accounts which still have at least a temporal *telos*, i.e. human freedom.

Now, Taylor does incorporate the modern insight into the "creative" as part of an historical reconstruction of what he calls the ethics of authenticity, but he does so in an account of eighteenth-century German Romanticism's shifting the "human centre of gravity" from

---

4   For development of this view, see Foster (1935).

logos to *poiesis*: "The artist becomes in some way the paradigm case of the human being as agent..." And, later, "no longer defined... by *mimesis* of reality... art is understood now more in terms of creation" (Taylor, 1992, p. 62). By contrast, as I have been attempting to show, Oakeshott incorporates the idea of the creative into his entire account of the structure of all experiential reality, and, in turn, in his accounts of appropriate and skilful activity in all aspects of life.

In the end, Taylor is simply more Hegelian than Oakeshott in characterizing human beings as rationally purposive beings, and in articulating forms of community congenial to rational purposiveness. Although both Oakeshott and Taylor are respectful of the Hegelian theme of "social-situatedness" of the individual, their differences on individual–community relationships have to do with the fact that Oakeshott shows more influence of the Hobbesian ("Will and Artifice") paradigm of thought and its emphasis on the importance of authority in preserving both order and individual moral autonomy: "It is Reason not Authority, which is destructive of individuality", wrote Oakeshott in introducing *Leviathan* (Oakeshott, 1975a, p. 63). Taylor, by contrast, in trying to rescue his ethics of authenticity from charges of egoism and narcissism, is led to strong defences of community as highly constitutive of individual identity, to the point of implying wholesale endorsement of what Oakeshott calls enterprise or teleocratic association, or association in terms of a common, substantive purpose.

Another twentieth-century thinker who shares some similarity with Oakeshott on what I am calling the "creative" is the economist and philosopher Frederich Hayek. (The two even corresponded in the 1960s when Oakeshott was formulating his account of teleocracy *vs* nomocracy.[5]) Detailed comparisons and contrasts of Oakeshott and Hayek on especially the critique of modern rationalist planning (including economic planning) have been made by others[6] and there is perhaps little new ground to break in this connection. They share a view of the limits of conscious intellect and an appreciation of the implicit rationality embodied in evolved or "spontaneous orders" (to use Hayek's terminology) in contrast to consciously crafted political, social, and economic institutions and organization, as well an appreciation of the importance of *general* rules of law to ground and channel "spontaneously" evolving orders such as markets based on the interplay of forces of demand and supply. In both cases this orientation derives from an appreciation of the *complexity* of both human experience and of the practical tasks facing large political and social entities.

---

5   Cited in Boyd and Morrison (2007, p. 102, note #1).
6   See, for example, Cheung (2014) and Boyd and Morrison (2007).

Insight into what I am calling the "creative" aspects of experience, in particular the awareness that the form and content of all human activity arises creatively, i.e. arises simultaneously, fluidly, and reciprocally, conditions their respective critiques of rationalism in morals, politics, and economics.

Perhaps what is most to be gained in comparing the two thinkers on the limits to rationalist planning is perspective on the different ways such critiques can be mounted, and how they re-enforce one another. For example, Hayek's psychological studies (Hayek, 1952) on limits of the human mind to know itself delve into areas of cognitive research which Oakeshott never addresses, but which support his philosophic skepticism. Perhaps the largest difference between the two thinkers is that Oakeshott remains even more skeptical than Hayek on the possibilities for human "progress" inherent in nurturing creative forces such as markets, and in the unwavering conviction that all civilizational achievements are highly complex and historically contingent and might have been otherwise, and could be again. Oakeshott's work is also generally more theoretically consistent than is Hayek's, given the diversity of subjects Hayek addressed over a lifetime, and in his pressing practical concern to foster markets and limited government under general rules of law.

It is appreciation of the "creative" in experience which sets off the thought of Oakeshott, Hayek (and even Taylor) from the "virtue ethics" of Alasdair MacIntyre. We might say that where Oakeshott has chosen to emphasize the creative side of the medieval inheritance, MacIntyre, following Aquinas, has followed its Aristotelian side by attempting to re-incorporate in morality a *telos* or final purpose tied to the performance of a human function (MacIntyre, 1981). While Oakeshott and MacIntyre do share an Aristotelian-like view of morality as skilful participation in inherited practice and traditions, Oakeshott's appreciation of the creative structure of experiential reality and the corresponding limits of conscious intellect to direct practical and moral life lead him, as we have seen, to reject any sort of teleological thinking in human affairs as simply confused. In defence of MacIntyre on this score, we might observe that his political realism leads him to reject the possibility that notions of a common purpose could ever intelligently and moderately be the basis for large modern states, and could only thrive in small, local associations as the basis for community in an instrumentalist liberal-capitalist age.

As for MacIntyre's account of the incommensurablity of modern versions of morality owing to competing conceptions of rationality (MacIntyre, 1988), we might observe that MacIntyre's account rests on an intellectual move that the early Oakeshott employed in establishing the separateness of various modalities of experience such as practice, science, and history, and which, it has been suggested, crystallized in Oakeshott's attempts in the 1920s to mediate between the claims of science and religion. This intellectual move is the invocation of the logical error of *ignoratio elenchi* or irrelevance. But for Oakeshott this move led to the view that there could be no scientific or rational proof or disproof of the practical claims of the Christian religion since the two were dealing with categorically different subject matters. By implication, this would entail a rejection as confused of the attempted Aquinian synthesis of Artistotelian reason and Christian revelation which MacIntyre extols as the most coherent and best model for regeneration of communities of rational morality in the contemporary world. And, more specifically, Oakeshott rejects as confused the attempt to inject "rationality" directly into morality by way of *telos* of shared, common purposes, natural or transcendental, grounded in an essentialist view of human beings as matrices of specifiable and hierarchically arranged functions, in favour of a more creative or Daoist-like and fluid conception of the individual self vis-à-vis the world, depending on the particular way the self is being active at any moment. In brief, all about all that Oakeshott and MacIntyre share is a view of the importance of evolved shared practices in the generation of the self and a concomitant rejection of Rawlsian-like accounts of "antecedently-situated" subjects or agents.

Oakeshott's differences with Leo Strauss here are profound since Strauss propounds the view that creativity, which he identifies with making, production, and the temporalizing of Being, has been the cause of "modern darkness" (Emberly and Cooper, 1993, pp. 65–66). Let us look closely at what Strauss is saying in this regard, and how Oakeshott's analysis differs from it, especially his critique of rationalism in morals and politics, extending back to Plato.

Strauss's viewpoint in this regard is that "modern derailments" have come from the confused "creative" attempt to conflate the theoretical, practical, and productive lives (which the ancient Greeks kept separate) by extending theorizing into the realm of the mutable and material, and privileging the latter over the former, with the effect of privileging productive and instrumentalist aims over questions of truth and right and wrong[7] (Strauss, 1952, p. 572). The real meaning of "creativity" for Strauss has been the historicizing of both Being and knowledge (Strauss, 1989, pp. 227–270), which he traces to at least

---

[7]   To see the contrast between Strauss and Oakeshott on these points, see my essay, "Theory and Practice in Oakeshott, Strauss and Voegelin", Coats (2012).

Descartes, obscuring the fact that voluntarist medieval thinkers such as Avicenna and Duns Scotus admitted the possibility of a theoretical knowledge of the strictly human, and, in the case of Scotus, even saw practical knowledge as an extension of theoretical knowledge (Lobkowicz, 1967, pp. 78–79). Strauss also insisted, like the exoteric Maimonides, that the philosophic and biblical ways of life were incompatible, especially creation and incarnation doctrines (Strauss, 1989, p. 260). However, another way of viewing all of this is to say, as we saw Andre de Muralt maintain in the first section of this paper, that modernity begins in the late medieval period with the voluntarist, nominalist univocal equation of divine and human willing.

To summarize here, the exoteric[8] Strauss uses the idea of creativity, not to distinguish a created from a crafted object, but to designate the entire view that thinking is making and dependent on history, or "the making of other men"; or in Kantian terms, that Reason understands that which it produces after a plan of its own; and to suggest this has been the source of modern ideological fanaticisms, modern instrumentalism, and modern public immorality.

In contrasting Oakeshott and Strauss on the origins of modern, rationalist ideological thinking we might summarily say the following. For (the exoteric) Strauss it is an outcome of a misguided, enthusiastic, "creative" attempt to extend the certainty of rational, knowledge into the realm of human mutability and time, and turn knowing into making; for Oakeshott it is a consequence of failure to perceive the creative structure of experiential reality through overestimation of the powers of conscious intellect, a development incipient as well in Platonic rationalism and its view of creation as imitative copying of antecedently conceived models, including models for reforming cities (Oakeshott, 1962, pp. 219–221). And in defence of Oakeshott on this point, one might cite the ancient Daoist critique of Mohist and Confucian rationalist attempts to "live by precept", a critique in no way influenced by a creationist and incarnationist religious symbolism. Oakeshott (like the Daoist writers he occasionally cites in footnotes to his critique of rationalism) proceeds by clear-sighted inspection of the basis for skill and balance in all activity, one reason he is appreciative of Aristotelian *phronesis* as a form of knowing. One might also observe, in criticism of Strauss's narrative on this point, that its implication is an

---

8   Stanley Rosen (1987, pp. 125–126) argues by logical implication that Strauss's defence of Greek rationalist philosophy is a salutary rhetorical posture, and that Strauss's own views are closer to those of Kant and Nietzsche. That claim is to one side of this paper's argument which simply engages Strauss's critique of creativity at face value.

indictment as well of the empirical side of all of modern science, a development which in combination with its Greek rationalist inheritance has arguably achieved deep insights into knowledge of physical reality, insights which Greek rationalist science could never have achieved *by itself*, given its elitist denigration of the material realm.

What Oakeshott and Strauss may be said to have in common in this connection is the view that *theoria*, or the activity of understanding and explaining, has an oblique relationship to practical (political and moral) activity, although less oblique for Plato and Strauss than for Oakeshott. In Straussian terms, "theory" for Oakeshott still remains more "seeing" than "making", in spite of Oakeshott's recognition of the creative character of experiential reality; philosophy for Oakeshott is not practice or production, and "the theorist of conduct" is not a "doer" (Oakeshott, 1975, p. 35).

By way of rehearsing this paper's themes I offer the following summary. I have articulated a point of view about the creative or dynamic tension of Western civilization which is especially congenial for characterizing the lifework of the twentieth-century English philosophical essayist, Michael Oakeshott. It is the tension between its Greek and biblical inheritances as historically mediated by those consummate pragmatists, the Romans and neo-Romans, who couldn't see the contradictions and kept trying to synthesize them, quintessentially in Aquinas. This tension is that between the Greek rationalist view of the primacy of logic in discerning an eternal, teleologically ordered cosmos, and a biblical, creationist account of the universe privileging temporality, will, and contingency, a tension manifest in the rational and empirical aspects of modern science, for example. I have suggested that Oakeshott's work is a rather unique take on this tension, in that it uses philosophic reason to identify the constructivist structure of all experiential reality as creative or poetic; and then uses this creative structure as a basis for his contingent preferences with regard to a plurality of subjects from morality, politics, and art, to philosophic and historical theorizing. I have tried to illustrate *both* the cogency of this large narrative for understanding the Western intellectual and social progression from unity and compactness to increasing differentiation and plurality, *as well as* its aptness in providing a degree of unity for Oakeshott's wide-ranging *opus*.

One practical implication of this paper's argument is that the modern and post-modern ascendency of the pole of creative differentiation in this dynamic tension may have reached its apex in the anarchic rush to "validate all difference" and now calls out for the reappearance of its opposite, if the animating tension of the West is not to be drained. Arguably, Oakeshott's account of "the creative" in human experience provides a sustainable and cogent view for a unified diversity grounded in a theoretically satisfying narrative of historically evolved forms generating identity and meaning from the sheer flux of contingency and particularity.

References

Bhuta, N. (2015) "The Mystery of the State: State concept, state theory and state making in Schmitt and Oakeshott", in Dyzenhaus, D. & Poole, T. (eds.) *Law, Liberty and the State*, pp. 18–19, Cambridge: Cambridge University Press.

Boucher, D. (2012) "Oakeshott in the context of British Idealism", in Podoksik, E. (ed.) *The Cambridge Companion to Oakeshott*, pp. 259–268, Cambridge: Cambridge University Press.

Boyd, R. & Morrison, J.A. (2007) "F.A. Hayek, Michael Oakeshott, and the Concept of Spontaneous Order", in Hunt, L. & McNamara, P. (eds.) *Liberalism, Conservatism and Hayek's Idea of Spontaneous Order*, New York: Palgrave Macmillan.

Cheung, C. (2014) "The Critique of Rationalism and the Defense of Individuality", *Cosmos & Taxis*, Vol. 1, 3.

Coats, W.J. (2012) "Theory and Practice in Oakshott, Strauss and Voegelin", in Coats, W.J. & Cheung, C.-Y., *The Poetic Character of Human Activity*, Lanham, MD: Lexington Books.

Dihle, A. (1982) *The Theory of Will in Classical Antiquity*, Berkeley, CA: University of California Press.

Emberly, P. & Cooper, B (eds.) (1993) *Faith and Political Philosophy: The Correspondence between Leo Strauss and Eric Voegelin, 1934–1964*, University Park, PA: Pennsylvania State University Press.

Foster, M.B. (1934) "The Christian Doctrine of Creation and the Rise of Modern Natural Science", *Mind*, Vol. 43 (Oct.), p. 464, note #1.

Foster, M.B. (1935) *The Political Philosophies of Plato and Hegel*, p. 138, Oxford: Clarendon Press.

Hayek, F. (1952) *The Sensory Order: An Inquiry into the Foundation of Theoretical Psychology*, London: Routledge.

Lobkowicz, N. (1967) *Theory and Practice: History of a Concept from Aristotle to Marx*, Notre Dame, IN: University of Notre Dame Press.

MacIntyre, A. (1981) *After Virtue*, Notre Dame, IN: University of Notre Dame Press.

MacIntyre, A. (1988) *Whose Justice: Which Rationality?*, Notre Dame, IN: University of Notre Dame Press.

Maimonides, M. (1963) *The Guide of the Perplexed*, Pines, S. (trans.), Chicago, IL: University of Chicago Press.

deMuralt, A. (1991) *L'Enjeu de la Philosophie Medievale*, p. 39 (my translation), Leiden: E.J. Brill.

Oakeshott, M. (1933) *Experience and Its Modes*, Cambridge: Cambridge University Press.

Oakeshott, M. (1967) "Learning and Teaching", in Peters, R.S. (ed.) *The Concept of Education*, pp. 156–176, London: Routledge.

Oakeshott, M. (1975a) *Hobbes on Civil Association*, Berkeley, CA: University of California Press.

Oakeshott, M. (1975b) *On Human Conduct*, Oxford: Claredon Press.

Oakeshott, M. (1962) *Rationalism in Politics and Other Essays*, London: Methuen and Co. Ltd.

Podoksik, E. (2013) "From Difference to Fragmentation", in Henkel, M. & Lembcke, O. (eds.) *Praxis und Politk – Michael Oakeshott im Dialog*, pp. 101–104, Tübingen: Mohr Siebeck.

Podoksik, E. (2015) "Neo-Kantianism and George Simmel's Interpretation of Kant, *Modern Intellectual History*, September 2015, pp. 1–26.

Rickert, H. (1924) *Kant als Philosoph der Modernen Kultur*, p. 150 (my translation), Tübingen: Mohr Siebeck.

Rosen, S. (1987) *Hermeneutics as Politics*, New York: Oxford University Press.

Strauss, L. (1952) "On Collingwood's Philosophy of History", *The Review of Metaphysics*, Vol. 5, 4.

Strauss, L. (1989) *The Rebirth of Classical Political Rationalism*, Pangle, T. (ed.), Chicago, IL: University of Chicago Press.

Taylor, C. (1992) *The Ethics of Authenticity*, Cambridge, MA: Harvard University Press.

Two

Michael Oakeshott, Modernity, and the "Creative"

"In recent times... [t]he Platonic understanding of the activity of copying ideal models... has been overshadowed by a concept of 'creative' activity..." — Michael Oakeshott, 1959.

There have been attempts to characterize the post-war works of the twentieth-century English political philosopher, Michael Oakeshott, as "post-modernist", since at least Richard Rorty's 1979 (mis)appropriation of Oakeshott's image of the "conversation of mankind" for Rorty's own highly relativistic epistemology.[1] More recently Efraim Podoksik has argued that Oakeshott is best understood as a participant in the early twentieth-century German conversation over the increasing diversity and plurality of modernity, advocating a radically pluralist or "fragmentationist" view of human experience and activity, and abandoning his earlier Idealist view of diversity as experiential modality of the whole.[2] This paper will advance the view that the most satisfactory account of Oakeshott's entire corpus will see it as remaining within modernity by providing a minimally unified account

---

[1] Richard Rorty (1979). On Rorty's co-option of Oakeshott's "conversation" metaphor, see Leslie Marsh (2005).

[2] My account differs with the account of Efraim Podoksik (2003, 2013) who argues that Oakeshott provides no philosophical basis for modern, radical plurality, and that, for Oakeshott, modernity can only be accounted for from a practical, not speculative, standpoint. My account also differs from the view of Stephen Turner (2005) in his lengthy review of Terry Nardin's book that it is a mistake to treat Oakeshott's account of experiential modality as essentially the same from *Experience and Its Modes* (1933) to *On Human Conduct* (1975).

of experiential diversity in the form of an insight about the poetic or creative character of all human experience.

Additionally, this paper will argue that if the term "modernity" is taken roughly to be the culture and practice of Western civilization from the late Renaissance to the twentieth century, then Michael Oakeshott may be viewed as an articulator of what is arguably its animating centre—the increasing recognition of, and reflection on, the creative (or poetic) character of human experience and activity, from medieval voluntarist/nominalist theology to Renaissance self-creation to non-teleological science to Kantian self-legislating morality.

"Modernity" has typically been identified as the increasing differentiation and fragmentation in culture and knowledge of the more unified medieval European outlook, and the concomitant claims for the relative autonomy of a plurality of compartmentalized activities and fields of knowledge, including the moral autonomy of the "sovereign" individual.[3] This paper argues that Oakeshott's account of the "poetic" or creative character of human experience provides a logical unity for proliferation of cultural and epistemological plurality and diversity of the Western world (especially) of the past five centuries or so.[4] In particular, this paper develops the theme that Oakeshott's comprehensive work provides a very intellectually satisfying basis for a unified account of modern diversity by showing how human knowledge

---

[3] See, for example, the tenth chapter ("Kritizismus und Moderne Weltaushaung") of Heinrich Rickert, *Kant als Philosoph der Modernen Kultur* (1924, pp. 139–150). There are, of course, problems with this neo-Kantian narrative which largely reflect the concerns of nineteenth-century and early twentieth-century German philosophic and literary minds. A strong case could also be made that the spread of monotheism, Cartesianism, the scientific method, the democratic egalitarian *ethos*, and the modern state have all led to increasing cultural homogeneity. For a dramatic instance contrast Aristotle's typology of three true constitutional forms with the modern democratic view (since Rousseau) that there is only one legitimate constitutional form. As we proceed, it may turn out that this German narrative is most apt in the realm of knowledge claims. For contrast, see also Louis Dupré (1993, p. 249), who argues that modernity has become a universal project and "the predicate of a unified world culture". Rickert called in 1924 for a new synthesis of knowledge which could account for the "many-sidedness" ("*Vielseitigkeit*") of realty, a new unity of knowledge achieved without any (regressive) loss to the fullness of cultural diversity.

[4] Insight into the creative or poetic character of human experience and activity could come from sources other than Jewish and Christian religious narratives. See, saliently, the case of Chinese Daoism, particularly the work *Chuang-tzu* (which Oakeshott drew upon in his critique of modern Rationalism). This theme is developed in various essays in *The Poetic Character of Human Activity* by Wendell J. Coats, Jr. and Chor-yung Cheung.

and skill evolve creatively, with neither form nor content of experience occupying a privileged position over the other. The unified account of modern diversity distinguishes Oakeshott's approach from (1) post-modernist "fragmentationist" accounts of diversity; the recognition of the role of the creative character of human experience distinguishes Oakeshott's approach from (2) pre-modernist (whether ancient, medieval, or contemporary) teleological accounts of diversity as error or idiosyncrasy.

The argument will proceed in stages. The first stage will be to summarize the characteristics of a created object as it arose in Western religious discourse and theology and was translated into other idioms. The second stage of the argument will be to show how Oakeshott's work reflects the understanding of the creative character of human experience, and in what ways it gives a unified account of the plurality of human activities. The third stage of the argument will be to pursue some ramifications of this understanding in Oakeshott's political views, especially. Finally, the ways in which Oakeshott can be considered as "anti-modern" will be briefly touched on.

I. A Created versus a Crafted Object

This section draws heavily on the thought of the English political philosopher, Michael Foster, with whose work Oakeshott was familiar and had reviewed, especially Foster's 1935 book, *The Political Philosophies of Plato and Hegel*[5] which analyses the blindnesses about the

---

[5] Michael B. Foster (1934, 1935). On the connections among creativity, will, and contingency, I have also relied upon (the only English language work of) German scholar Albrecht Dihle, *The Theory of Will in Classical Antiquity*; and upon Hannah Arendt's summaries of the medieval voluntarist Duns Scotus in the second volume ("Willing") of *The Life of the Mind*. See, also, Dupre's very competent articulation of the implications of medieval nominalist theology in *Passage to Modernity*, pp. 15–41, which draws fruitfully upon French scholarship, in particular the untranslated work of Andre de Muralt who makes a sustained argument in his work, *L'Enjeu de la Philosophie Medievale* (1991) that the modern view of infinite freedom of the will begins (not with Descartes or Kant but) in the thirteenth century in thought of Scotus (and Ockham). See, especially p. 39: "The rehabilitation of medieval thought... permits us to consider the evolution of Western civilization as a continuity without a break. In particular it is between 1250 and 1350, very precisely, that the premise of the contemporary intellectual situation appears (as well as the decline of a unified philosophic conception of possible human knowledge)... a formalized, univocal knowledge which pretends to reign exclusively today" (my translation). Muralt is also lucid in showing the connection between modern liberal conceptions of liberty as freedom to act short of harm to another, and Ockhamite conceptions of

structure of reality of both thinkers for failing to achieve (Plato) or incorporate (Hegel) the empirical insights about reality implicit in the creation stories of ancient Jewish and Christian religious texts. Since this paper is suggesting that the animating centre (both speculatively and practically) of Western "modernity" has been the increasingly explicit idea of the "creative", it is important to understand the meaning of the term and how it differs from the Greek Rationalist, ontological-dualist viewpoint of Plato and Aristotle which has been so influential on the Western mind following the Aquinian synthesis.

As is generally known, in the ancient Greek Rationalist worldview, both form and matter are given eternally; the essence of any object is its "detachable" form which is known by intellection; matter adds nothing positive to essence or form; and both thinking and making are purposive and involve discovering and coping pre-existing forms or models. Even Plato's divine craftsman in the *Timaeus* only moulds or informs pre-existing matter into pre-existing forms. By contrast, the account of cosmological "creation" in the ancient Hebrew and early Christian texts[6] entails the idea that an act of creation is not purposive in the Greek sense, that is, it is not directed toward a distinctively conceived and antecedently existing end or form in advance of the act of execution of wilful creation; and, by implication, in creation and in a created (versus a crafted) object there is no intellectively graspable form distinguished from its accidental embodiment. Several more implications follow. Creation is an act of will which can exceed regulations prescribed by reason. Contingency is an important aspect of created objects (including human beings), that is, their "accidental" embodiments are not necessitated by, nor can be deduced from, their form or idea. And, finally, there can be no degrees of being in creation as in the

---

authority as an external limit to infinite individual freedom, distinguished from older views of both Augustine and Aristotle that human willing is naturally directed to what is good. For Scotus and Ockham both divine and human will are pure, unlimited, indeterminate power without finality (pp. 80–81). See also, in this connection, Dupré (1993), who is explicitly critical of Oakeshott for dating the individualist political orientation only to late modernity.

6 Arendt (1978) suggests, citing work of Hans Jonas, that the Christian doctrine of creation *ex nihilo* evolved when the early Church fathers confronted the Greek idea of Being (for which there is no Hebrew word) and posited nothingness as its opposite, thus amplifying the original biblical account. This may be overstated, as one can find assertions in ancient Hebrew texts that God created the heavens and earth "not from things that already were". See II Maccabeus, 7:28 in *The Apocrypha*, any edition. See, also, Dihle (1981, pp. 1–19) on the dialogue between Greek and Jewish cosmology reaching back to at least the first two centuries, C.E.

Greek concept of *ousia*: if something is created *ex nihilo*, "it must be entirely present as soon as it has ceased to be wholly absent".[7]

It is instructive at this point, by way of further illumination of the differences between a created and crafted object, to consider the case of modern political sovereignty contrasted with the case of the political craftsman in Plato's *Republic*. The ideas of the state (versus the *polis*), as articulated by Hobbes[8] and Rousseau[9] especially, requires the presence and maintenance of a sovereign will which creates or imposes upon itself its own constitutional form (a creative act definitionally), contrasted with the account of a founder or constitutional craftsman in the formation (or "in-formation") of the *polis* of *The Republic*. The modern state is a created or artificial (Hobbes' usage) body because (1) it is the product of a sovereign will which informs itself; (2) it is informed by no distinct previously existing purpose; (3) and therefore its essence cannot be separated from its existence by philosophic intellect, and used as an external measure against which to criticize existing states, which by implication can only be judged historically. Additionally, since the state's existence cannot be separated from its essence, its realization (as in the case of Anselm's "ontological proof" for the existence of God) inhers in it, or completes it, in a way Plato has Socrates explicitly deny to the ideal *polis* of *The Republic*.[10]

By way of summary of this section of the argument, I'll simply note again that this paper is advancing the notion that Western civilization of the past five centuries or so ("modernity") is (1) characterized by the

---

7   Foster (1934, p. 464 note 1). Although he does not cite it (perhaps assuming it as common knowledge in 1935) most of Foster's account of creation vs. craft (*techne*) was worked out by early Church fathers such as Athanasius and Augustine in their dialogue with classical dualism. For a detailed account see Charles Cochrane (1944).

8   The case is less pure for Hobbes than for Rousseau since it only fits without qualification for Hobbes when the constitutional form chosen is democracy, a hypothetical possibility he enumerates in *Leviathan*. The case of Hegel is ambiguous since for him the essence of sovereignty is the state's organic unity which is not a product of creative will.

9   Even Rousseau's account in *The Social Contract* is somewhat qualified since he tries to reintroduce the ancient claim for the founding role of wisdom by way of the extra-constitutional "Legislator" who nurtures wise choices amongst the people prior to their self-creative political act. No human activity can be purely creative, carefully speaking, since the "creator" always requires some materials which already exist, or were produced by someone else.

10   "'But in heaven,' I said, 'perhaps a pattern is laid up for the man who wants... to found a city within himself... It doesn't make any difference whether it is or will be somewhere'", Plato (1968, p. 225 (592b)).

increasing liberation from Greek intellectual forms, modern Enlightenment rationalism to the contrary notwithstanding; (2) that this liberation has been led by the largely implicit spread of the idea of the
"creative" in both thought and action; (3) that the idea of "the creative"
provides a speculative, integrative unity for the appreciation of the
concomitant spread of diversity and plurality; and (4) that Oakeshott's
work may be seen as a rather original account of diversity in unity
(beginning with his version of how modality arises in human experience) which separates Oakeshott from the post-modernist embrace of
an anarchic "fragmentation" of culture (anarchic, that is, if the deconstruction of inherited hierarchy leads to the validation of all
difference).[11]

II. Oakeshott and the "Creative"
Character of Experience

This section of my argument will attempt to show the influence of the
"creative" in Oakeshott's comprehensive work, even at points where he
may not have been fully aware of it. (That is, if Oakeshott saw rather
clearly the structure of reality, and if reality reflects creative aspects,
then Oakeshott could have incorporated these aspects in his
descriptions of reality without yet fully recognizing them at any
particular time as "creative".) In particular, let us look at Oakeshott's
initial account of experience and its modes, and its subsequent modification to include the modility of artistic creation; at Oakeshott's
critique of modern Rationalism in morals and politics; and at
Oakeshott's account of theoretical perspective of "history", or as he
later called it, "theorizing contingency".[12]

In a fashion similar to Hobbes' claim in *Leviathan* that nature is
God's art, one might argue that Oakeshott's account of experiential

---

[11] On the distinction between existential "differentiation" and existential
"fragmentation" see Podoksik (2013) "From Differentiation to Fragmentation", in *Praxis and Politik*, especially pp. 97–101, who argues that Oakeshott
falls in the camp of those who identify modern plurality with "fragmentation" rather than unity in diversity. Against this view see the conclusion to
this paper. For an instance of what I call "anarchic fragmentation", consider
Giles Deleuze, *Difference and Repetition* (1968).

[12] Oakeshott's initial Idealist account of experience and its modalities is in
Experience and Its Modes (1933). His critique of modern rationalism is in
Rationalism in Politics and Other Essays (1962), which also contains the long
essay, "The Voice of Poetry in the Conversation of Mankind", where for the
first time Oakeshott treats aesthetic experience as a separate modality or
voice. The account of "Theorizing Contingency" occurs in the first essay of
On Human Conduct (1975).

reality accords with the view that it has the features of a created object. Consider the following. For Oakeshott, all we know and experience, hence all that is real, is a present world of ideas mediated on some principle which in the interaction with some substantial claims generates an identifiable and particular subject matter distinguishable from other modifications or modalities of the totality of experience, i.e. reality. Furthermore these various modalities of the totality of experience (such as practice, science, history) do not add up to or constitute the totality of experiential reality. Is this not a variation on the view that a created object exists completely once it ceases to be absent, and that there are no degrees of being as in the Greek Rationalist doctrine of *ousia* or substance?

The way in which various modalities of the totality of experience evolve in Oakeshott's account also accords with the difference between a created and crafted object, the former of which has no antecedently existing form or purpose separable by intellect from its "informed" content. For Oakeshott the various modalities evolve "creatively" (not his term in 1933) in the sense that they arise over time in a fluid interaction between their distinctive form and content, neither able to assimilate or extinguish the other, and both contributing equally to the genesis of a distinctive modal identity. Although it is true that Oakeshott treats "will" as a form of thought or judgment, his account of the evolution of modalities of experience has characteristics of wilfully created objects, including the implication that *contingency* is an essential aspect of these various identities because their content cannot be deduced from their form, and therefore their existence is integral (not accidental) to their enduring identity. This is the reason why Oakeshott can be said to provide a speculative or unified basis for the plurality or diversity of the world, and the reason why he says that the number of experiential modalities is hypothetically limitless. Modalities of reality arise contingently and historically in the interplay between their form and content, between a *how* and *what* of experience, and what is similar in their unfolding diversity is the structure of their evolution which is creative, not intellectively "informative" as in the Greek Rationalist, ontologically-dualist cosmology, nor anarchically random or fragmented as in some post-modernist accounts.

When Oakeshott revisits this account of experience in "The Voice of Poetry..." to amend the place of aesthetic experience, the role of the "creative" in his thought becomes even more explicit, with poetic or aesthetic experience now described as experience in which *how* something is said or done, and *what* is said or done are momentarily unified or one. In my view, Oakeshott implies here that the creative structure of all experiential reality is most clearly revealed in poetic or aesthetic experience, even though it is often repressed in more prosaic modalities such as practice and science. Nevertheless, these modalities of experience also evolve creatively, the reason why they can only address one another obliquely and conversationally. There is no common subject matter in experience, and each modality is autonomous in its own domain where it creates its own "images".

The creative structure of experiential reality is also the basis of Oakeshott's critique of a prosaic hyper-rationalism in morals and politics—rationalism presuming that these are separable ideals and models which can be detached from the activities which generated them, and irrelevantly applied (both to themselves and) to other activities, at loss of skill and moral balance. Carefully speaking, so called "universal" methods and ideologies only create new, hybrid subject matters when "universally" and indiscriminately applied, and may have only the most tangential relevance to the practical problems they are intended to solve. In balanced skills and moralities, the role of intellect is a critic not instigator of action, except during times of crisis and emergency.

Another aspect of Oakeshott's life work which reflects the creative structure of experiential reality is his detailed investigation of a theoretical method capable of making intelligible "meaning" in human conduct. The pivot of this method is recognition of the importance of *contingency* in human affairs as a definitional characteristic of created (vs. crafted) objects or creatures, where contingency is understood as that which could have been otherwise, and which is integral to their identities, rather than merely accidental.

Oakeshott has argued in his early writing that modalities of experience understood as arrested views of the totality of experience could not feasibly be ordered in terms of degrees of coherence, but I would like to argue that they could be roughly ordered in terms of extent to which they reflect the creative or poetic character of experiential reality. In this light, the activity of writing history and "theorizing contingency" can be seen as more poetic than the arrests[13] in experience he calls science and practice (though less so than artistic experience). How, then, does the activity of writing history reflect the creative character of experiential reality?

"History" for Oakeshott, in accounts spanning a half-century, is a theoretical language for making intelligible "goings-on" or events by putting them in a story with no beginning and no end, in which they

---

[13] Oakeshott continues to employ the term "arrests" (in the progression of inquiry into postulates of intelligibility) in his later (1975) work, *On Human Conduct*.

"touch" or elucidate one another by being shown to emerge from one another in detailed and incremental mediation. It is distinguished from teleological, scientific, and organic perspectives, and definitionally postulates "contingency" as integral rather than incidental to its subject matter, and, in fact, Oakeshott calls the activity of theorizing a substantive event in human conduct "theorizing contingency"; it is said to be a way of explaining human events "without explaining them away" by incorporating an extraneous explanatory principle such as a "law" of behaviour. Like the early twentieth-century German school of "Verstehen" it is concerned with capturing human *meaning*, but for Oakeshott it exists only as a present world of ideas in the mind of the historian, not as an account of things "as they really were". By the standards of creativity (and created objects) we have elucidated thus far, "history" is a highly creative activity — it is entirely present and it is predicated on (to employ medieval terminology) the equal importance of *existence* and *essence*, hence its focus on the contingent as something which could have been otherwise, and which cannot be philosophically deduced, from, or necessitated by, its idea or essence. (Oakeshott's account of the equality of existence and essence might be viewed as a secularized equivalent of Scotian "univocity", although Oakeshott nowhere acknowledges Duns Scotus.)

III. Implications

In his brief, admiring 1935 review of Michael Foster's *The Political Philosophies of Plato and Hegel*, Oakeshott called it an original and subtle exploration not only of Plato's *Republic* and Hegel's *Philosophie des Rechts*, but an illumination of "the whole history of political philosophy", and in particular of the "fundamental similarities and differences which join and divide the ancient and modern way of thinking about political problems".[14] In that work Foster criticizes Hegel's attempt to depict reality for failing to assimilate the insights implicit in biblical creative accounts and in the subsequent Christian doctrine of creation *ex nihilo*, i.e. for failing to appreciate fully the claims of modern empiricism and modern subjectivism. It is unfortunate that Oakeshott did not engage with Foster's arguments (except to praise them generally) for this might have compelled him to think and say more explicitly than he ever did about where exactly he stood in his subsequent attempts to straddle what he later called the philosophic

---

[14] Reprinted from *Cambridge Review* in Luke O'Sullivan (ed.) *The Concept of a Philosophical Jurisprudence: Essays and Reviews, 1926–51* (Exeter, Imprint Academic, 2007, pp. 126–127).

traditions of "Will and Artifice" and "the Rational Will". But perhaps we can attempt this for him here briefly.

Foster's criticism of Hegel's philosophy is that it:

> shows no trace of the metaphysics of the will implicit in the Judaic doctrines of the Creation and the Law, which entails the recognition that contingency is essential to nature, positivity to law, and will to the perfection of man...[15]

Let us explore, by a way of making some judgments about Oakeshott and "modernity" (vs. "pre- and post-modernity") his relation to these three ideas enumerated by Foster: (1) contingency, (2) positivity, and (3) will. Before taking up this exploration, I should say why I think Oakeshott should be considered first and foremost a political theorist rather than an expositor of ontology, or epistemology, and, hence, why it is appropriate to assess his relationship to "modernity" primarily by way of his accounts of political "things".

Beginning with his first major work, *Experience and Its Modes*, the level of generality at which Oakeshott discourses is arguably most appropriate to the relationship between thought and action ("theory-practice"), and it is on this relationship that (arguably) he makes his most insightful and startling observations, such as the (for the most part) irrelevance of philosophy to practical life, the irrelevance of history to the practical past, the irrelevance of one modality of experience to another, the irrelevance of art to truth, and so on. This level of generality seems most appropriate, by its middling level of abstraction, to questions about the relationship between what might be called ideals and action, a focus and subject matter which is the stuff of political theory. It is true that Oakeshott does occasionally address more *specific* epistemological questions, and more general ontological questions, but, arguably, these are not deeply explored, and are usually tangential to "theory-practice" issues, with the exception of Oakeshott's late historiographic essays. The irrelevance of various modalities of experience to

---

15 Foster (1935, p. 138). Paul Franco (1999) has defended Hegel against Foster's charges, arguing that Hegel provides a "radical and self-consistent expression of the modern emphasis on the primacy of the will". That is, Franco argues that Hegel's idea of human freedom as rational self-determination brings out better than Foster's "what we understand by freedom and why we find it valuable", because it gives expression to our fulfilment as rational, purposive beings. But Foster (and others like him) would simply reply that Hegel's account of the Rational Will necessitates for fulfilment intellectual capacities not available to the majority of non-philosophic individuals, and also fails to do justice to the mystery and variety of human ends and purposes. On Foster's view, both Hegel and Aristotle overestimate the capacities of even philosophic human intellect.

one another as incomplete views of the totality of experience, for example, is most germane and appropriate (given its middling level of abstraction) to the culturally institutionalized relation among these various modalities, a fitting subject for political theory rather than for theories of being or knowing.

Now, if I am permitted to treat Oakeshott as first and foremost a political theorist, in what sense is he a political theorist of "modernity" and what light do Foster's three questions (contingency, legal positivity, and will) throw on this assessment? Incontestably, a salient moral and political development of Western "modernity" of the past five centuries has been the achievement and cultivation of the "individual", and I should like to take it as a litmus test of evidence of "modernity". This development reaches its speculative apex in the philosophic idealism of the German philosophers Kant and Hegel ("Das Ich" is the Absolute), and its claim that the individual ego is in its essence spiritually free and capable of liberation through will from antecedent genetic and cultural conditioning, evident in the human capacity for wilful suicide (Hegel),[16] or the incapacity to follow self-legislated moral law (Kant). Now, where did Oakeshott stand on the importance and desirability and cultivation of individuality and the political arrangements to favour it?

Oakeshott says in his own name as far back as *Experience and Its Modes* that the interesting question for him concerned degrees of individuality attained.[17] On this view the only absolute individual is the whole, or the universe as a whole—all other claims to individuality are merely designated or built upon unexamined postulates or assumptions. The historical individual is not the scientific individual, is not the practical individual, and so on. This means that what is typically called individuality by most people is the practical individual, the self-contained unique self which must be designated or presupposed if practical action bridging the gap between "what is" and "what ought to be" is to be possible at all. And within the realm of practical experience, where religion, politics, ethics, economics occur, Oakeshott clearly shows a contingent preference for "individualist" political arrangements, perhaps because they reflect more purely the presuppositions of practical experience in general, i.e. that there be a world of discrete individual entities as an enduring condition for "practice" to continue to be possible.

---

[16] "I possess the members of my body, my life, only so long as I will to possess them. An animal cannot maim or destroy itself, but a man can", Hegel, (1952, p. 43). See, for development of this theme, Jeffrey Church (2012).

[17] Oakshott (1933, pp. 151, 44).

Summarizing Hobbes' views in his 1946 introduction to *Leviathan*, Oakeshott observed that "it is Reason not Authority which is destructive of Individuality".[18] Three years later in his review of J.D. Mabbott's *The State and the Citizen*, Oakeshott argued that the individual was a socially constituted institution (which would collapse like a body in a vacuum if separated from the social world), but that it would be disastrous to apply such philosophic insights directly to practical existence.[19] In my view Oakeshott is implying that there is no satisfactory philosophic defence of the self-contained individual outside of practical experience,[20] and that the social and legal institutions nurturing the existence of such selves are simply the outcome of many historic choices that might have been otherwise, but that we have grown to like and might like to keep. And Oakeshott's various "defences" of political institutions associated with classical Liberalism such as rule of formal law and decentralized political and economic arrangements reflect an appreciation of both practical individuality and the creative character of experience in general.

Thus, on Foster's three criticisms of Hegelian philosophy—contingency, legal positivity, and will—Oakeshott would appear to have improved on Hegel (in Foster's eyes). Both Oakeshott's account of the character of experience as a whole and the structure of practical experience reflect creative aspects. Experience for Oakeshott is like a wilfully created object in that as a world of ideas it is fully present—each modality of experience is a world of ideas which asserts itself completely as a version of the whole—there are no degrees of being in experience and reality. Additionally, various modes of experience evolve historically with no preconceived idea of where they are going as would be the case in a crafted, teleological universe. (Recall Oakeshott says that the universe as whole has no value.)[21] The modality of practical experience, the realm of *designated* individuality and of questions of value and worth, is navigated best in its most poetic moments, avoiding the prosaic traps of excessive rationalism. And on political activity Oakeshott shows clear appreciation after 1946 for the importance of authority over rationality ("positivity in law") in his explorations on Hobbes. (If the number of creatively evolving modalities of experience is potentially limitless, then formal authority is the only sure basis for order as their proliferations increase.) His

---

[18] Oakeshott (1975, p. 63).

[19] Oakeshott (2007, p. 256).

[20] As David Boucher (2012) puts it, Oakeshott remained within the camp of Absolute Idealism against the camp of Personal Idealism and its conception of the reality of the finite self.

[21] Oakeshott (1933, p. 287).

account of non-instrumental civil association also provides latitude for diverse activities to arise creatively and be governed insofar as feasible by their own internal, evolved logic. Finally, Oakeshott's appreciation of the centrality of contingency in human affairs is evident in his construction of the presuppositions of practical existence, and in the articulation of a theoretical perspective ("theorizing contingency") capable of explaining an event in human conduct "without explaining it away". Individuality, for Oakeshott, may be an arrested and designated identity within the modality of practical experience, but it is one for which Oakeshott shows a clear contingent preference as a practical choice.

As for the plurality and diversity of "autonomous" realms of being associated with "modernity", Oakeshott's insights into the poetic or creative structure of human experiential reality arguably provide an integrated or unified perspective for accounting for their respective claims to autonomy. Historically evolving self-contained modalities of experience are theoretically limitless in number since their creative and contingent character makes it impossible for them to be deduced or necessitated from some antecedently existing form or idea, as in Hegel's various depictions in the successive and more coherent and comprehensive realizations of *Geist*. Nor is the poetic structure of experiential reality similar to *a priori* categories of the mind as in the Kantian account of experience — on Oakeshott's Absolute Idealist[22] view since there is nothing outside of conscious experience, the poetic structure of consciousness must be the structure of reality. That Oakeshott also depicts an abiding structure to experiential reality sets him off from post-modernist thinkers such as Derrida and Rorty as well. And that he insists on the importance of formal authority over mere power distances him as well from the "unmasking" reduction of political forms by neo-Nietzschean thinkers such as Foucault.[23]

---

[22] To weigh in on the issue of how completely Oakeshott stayed within the tradition of Absolute Idealism in his later works, it seems to me that the issue is not over growing philosophic scepticism — Idealism is based upon the skeptical premise that "truth is the whole", but the whole can never be known, and recedes when approached directly. Rather, the issue is whether the belief that philosophy as "experience for its own sake" can co-exist with Oakeshott's later claims that various practical activities could also be done for their own sake, activities such as patriotism, fishing, and friendship. If arrests in experience can be done for their own sake, ontologically speaking, this calls into question whether they are any longer arrests in experience.

[23] On the danger that a post-modern politics of identity and difference may "concern itself over policy issues, and ignore the conditions of legitimacy which are the foundation of limited politics", see Noel O'Sullivan (1993).

IV. Oakeshott as Anti-Modern
(and Anti-Post-Modern)

Before leaving this exploration of Oakeshott and "modernity", it is instructive to indicate briefly a salient sense in which Oakeshott does *not* fit into mainstream Western civilization of the past five centuries. This is its focus, both speculative and practical, on the primacy of practical experience, and, within it, the importance of cumulative "progress". Except to say that practical experience is unavoidable (though not, thereby, necessary) Oakeshott never makes concessions to its primacy in human life. Philosophy and poetry are viewed as intermittent escapes from the "deadliness" of practical experience, and expressions of the primary human impulse to behold rather than act or do. This is why Oakeshott can say that philosophy is experience for its own sake.[24] Additionally, philosophy is, for the most part, irrelevant to practical experience. And Oakeshott's account of scientific experience as quantitative experience cannot distinguish ancient Pythagorean science from modern science. His account does not acknowledge the advances in knowledge of physical reality made by modern empirical science in respecting the mystery of "created" matter by using logic and mathematics to talk *about* its probable movement and behaviour rather than attempting to give a "*logos*" of it.

In the end Oakeshott (like Heidegger in this instance) is simply too Augustinian to be considered a supporter of the prideful human attempt to master the world through rationalist techniques, and too skeptical to have any taste for its resentful project to reverse and correct for what are viewed as nature's inequalities and imperfections, *à la* Rawls. If I am correct that "modernity" has been about the increasing actualization of the "creative" in human experience, then Oakeshott will not follow it to the point of extending the infinite, creative subjectivity of German Idealism into the realm of political and social action in any sort of misguided, meliorist attempt to alter the fundamental conditions and assumptions making practical life possible as the focus of designated, discrete individuality. Oakeshott's bent is toward individual choice to appreciate and cultivate the poetic and ritualistic aspects of practical life which can be done for their own sake insofar as is meaningfully possible, and for intermittent escapes from practical existence whenever realistically possible. As for Oakeshott's "embracing" the radical plurality of the modern world, I do not see that

---

24 Oakeshott (1933, p. 83). For more on Oakeshott's aversion to the "primacy of practical life" viewpoint, see Wendell J. Coats, Jr., "Michael Oakeshott and Contemporary Political Philosophy", in Coats and Cheung (2012, pp. 79–98), and Kenneth B. McIntyre (pp. 187–192).

he ever modifies his early understanding that diversity be conceived as modalities of experience as a whole.[25] Whatever reconciliation is possible with this diversity occurs by *understanding* and *appreciating* the poetic or creative character of human experience, that is, by understanding that the form and content of its modalities arise simultaneously in consciousness and condition one another reciprocally, with neither more important than the other in establishing their identities.

References

Arendt, H. (1978) *The Life of the Mind*, pp. 125–156, New York: Harcourt Brace Jovanovich.

Boucher, D. (2012) "Oakeshott in the Context of British Idealism", in Podoksik, E. (ed) *The Cambridge Companion to Oakeshott*, pp. 259–265.

Church, J. (2012) *Infinite Antonomy*, pp. 32–33, University Park, PA: Pennsylvania State University Press.

Coats, W.J. & Cheung, C. (2012) *The Poetic Character of Human Activity*, pp. 79–98, Lanham, MD: Lexington Books.

Cochrane, C. (1944) *Christianity and Classical Culture*, Oxford: Oxford University Press.

Dihle, A. (1982) *The Theory of Will in Classical Antiquity*, Berkeley, CA: University of California Press.

Dupre, L. (1993) *Passage to Modernity*, p. 249, p. 272, n. 31, New Haven, CT: Yale University Press.

Foster, M.B. (1934) "The Christian Doctrine of Creation and the Rise of Modern Natural Science", *Mind*, Vol. 43, 172, pp. 446–468.

Foster, M.B. (1935) *The Political Philosophies of Plato and Hegel*, Oxford: Oxford University Press.

Franco, P. (1999) *Hegel's Philosophy of Freedom*, p. 186, New Haven, CT: Yale University Press.

Hegel, G.W.F (1952) *Philosophy of Right*, Knox, T.M. (ed.), p. 43, Oxford: Oxford University Press.

Marsh, L. (2005) "Contructivism and Relativism in Oakeshott", in Abel, C. & Fuller T. (eds.) *The Intellectual Legacy of Michael Oakeshott*, p. 251, Exeter: Imprint Academic.

McIntyre, K. (2004) *The Limits of Political Theory*, pp. 187–192, Exeter: Imprint Academic.

---

[25] "A view for which there is nothing beyond... diversity is one in which diversity is conceived in terms other than that of modality", Oakeshott (1933, p. 77, note 1). "...I do not know myself where to place an experience released altogether from modality...", Oakeshott (1962, p. 220). Oakeshott continued to refer to modal distinctions in his late work, *On History and Other Essays* (1983).

deMuralt, A. (1991) *L'Enjeu de la Philosophic Medievale*, Leiden: E.J. Brill.

Oakeshott, M.J. (1933) *Experience and Its Modes*, Cambridge: Cambridge University Press.

Oakeshott, M.J. (1975) *Hobbes on Civil Association*, Berkeley, CA: University of California Press.

Oakeshott, M.J. (1975) *On Human Conduct*, Oxford: Oxford University Press.

Oakeshott, M.J. (2007) Review of M.B. Foster, *The Political Philosophies of Plato and Hegel*, reprinted in O'Sullivan, L. (ed.) *The Concept of a Philosophical Jurisprudence: Essays and Reviews*, pp. 126–127, Exeter: Imprint Academic.

O'Sullivan, N. (1993) "Political Integration, the Limited State, and the Philosophy of Post Modernism", *Political Studies*, Vol. 14, pp. 41–42.

Plato (1968) *The Republic*, Bloom, A. (ed. & trans.), p. 225 (5926), New York: Basic Books.

Podoksik, E. (2013) "From Differentation to Fragmentation", in Henkel, M. & Lembcke, O. (eds.) *Praxis and Politik*.

Podoksik, E. (2003) *In Defense of Modernity*, pp. 3–33, Exeter: Imprint Academic.

Rickert, H. (1924) *Kant als Philosoph der Modernen Kultur*, Tübingen: Mohr-Siebeck.

Rorty, R. (1979) *Philosophy and the Mirror of Nature*, pp. 264, 318, 389, Princeton, NJ: Princeton University Press.

Turner, S. (2005) "The English Heidegger", *Philosophy of the Social Sciences*, Vol. 35, 3, pp. 353–368.

Three

Some Correspondences between Oakeshott's Critique of Rationalism & A.C. Graham's Account of "Spontaneity vs. Reason"

The impetus for this exploration comes from observation of the obvious debt owed by both of these thinkers to the ancient Chinese Daoist tradition of thought, especially the views in the fourth-century BCE composite work, *Chuang-tzu* or *Zhuangzi*. Although this debt is much greater in the case of A.C. Graham (a professional sinologist in addition to being a philosophic thinker), there is something to be gained in exploring the critique of Western Rationalism and its consequences for practical (religious, political, social, craft-like, and so on) living, found in both twentieth-century British thinkers. The aim here in this collection of essays on Michael Oakeshott is twofold — to get a fuller sense of Oakshott's debt to the worldview of *Chuang-tzu*, and to understand more fully (by way of comparison with Graham) what is entailed in Oakeshott's criticisms of Rationalism in moral and political life, especially.

A good way to proceed with this is to give a summary account of Graham's major arguments in his 1985 book, *Reason and Spontaneity*,[1] and then show their overlap with Oakeshott's critique of Rationalism

---

[1] Professor Angus Graham (1919–1991), philosopher and sinologist, was a foremost scholar and translator of ancient Chinese Daoist thought. He considered *Reason vs. Spontaneity* (1985) to be the best statement of his general philosophic view. For a glowing characterization of his scholarly influence, see the dedication to Khellberg and Ivanhoe (eds.) (1996).

in, especially, *Rationalism in Politics and Other Essays* (1962). The brunt of this exploration will be to show that Oakeshott's idea of a healthy and balanced moral and political life as one in which analytic intellect is the critic but not instigator of action, is supported and enriched by Graham's interpretation of the viewpoint of the Daoist composite work, *Chuang-tzu* (which Oakeshott quotes from in footnotes especially).[2]

Let us begin with some quotations from Graham's "Preface", which lays out the direction of his argument:

> The idea of this book is that we men of reason have been misunderstanding the relation between reason and spontaneity... that we have never fully come to terms with the thought that even our most deeply considered choices of ends are often (...always?) choices between goals which are themselves spontaneous.[3]
>
> ...if it is indeed the case that the basic choices are between conflicting spontaneous pulls, the balance of which shifts with changing awareness of self and situation, then the mere *obligation to be aware of things as they objectively are will commit me to prefer the goal to which I am drawn when most aware*. This suggests implications which we shall follow... through the themes of egoism and altruism, pleasure, creativity, the sacred, the relation between science and poetry, and between rationalism and irrationalism. (1985, p. vii, emphasis added)

Graham also observes, in this preface, that he intends to proceed by pursuing the ramifications from many angles of a single, simple idea: the predominant role of spontaneous (i.e. not the result of considered choice) activity in human conduct, and the importance for courses of action of being as "aware" as possible of self and situation. And he distinguishes his viewpoint from that of eighteenth- and early nineteenth-century Western Romanticism's praise of spontaneity for its intensity rather than its capacity to generate intelligent awareness and course of action.

Graham's basic orientation toward reason, which he says he owes to Chuang-tzu, is that analytic reason is to be employed just so much as use of it contributes to increased awareness of self and situation. He calls this the "Reason as Guide" approach and distinguishes it from the

---

[2] When Oakeshott and Graham wrote, "Chuang-tzu" was the conventional English rendering of the classic work, and could refer to both the work and the author(s). Contemporary scholarship now renders it as "Zhuang-zi". I have retained both renderings throughout, depending on context.

[3] Some interpreters read the *Chuang-tzu* as more skeptical and relativist than does Graham. For a discussion of some of the issues, see Eric Schwitzgebel (1996) "Zhuangzi's Attitude Toward Language and His Skepticism", in Paul Kjellberg and Philip J. Ivanhoe (eds.) *Essays on Skepticism, Relativism and Ethics in the Zhuangzi* (Albany, NY: State University of New York), especially pp. 86–88.

"Reason as Master" approach to living. Here is some of Graham's description of the subscriber to the view of "Reason as Master":

> In becoming a rational agent, I make an absolute break with my own spontaneity. I chose my means from the spontaneous outside or inside myself, but my ends come from God, reason, or a <u>fiat</u> of my own... On this view, "Be aware" is irrelevant to choices except in the preliminary collection of information. (*ibid.*, p. 151)

Graham then asks why it is that on "first becoming self-conscious we seem predisposed to the 'Reason as Master' position", to the claim for an "absolute divorce from the spontaneity of the animal"? To attempt a summary of his intricate and nuanced Western historical narrative covering the decline of teleological reasoning and of the spiritual, and the rise of causal explanation to explain the sub-rational, let us say Graham essentially argues that the rise of the autonomous individual gives birth to the view that it is itself the source of all its talents, except for its obscene or destructive ones:

> At the start... we objected to the doctrine of Original Sin for the inconsistency of ascribing the spontaneous in us to God when it is good and to our own nature when it is bad. *The person who submits to "Reason as Master" is guilty of the reverse error. When the forces which overwhelm him are creative he takes the whole credit*, when they are destructive he feels he is "not himself". (*ibid.*, p. 155, emphasis added)

For Graham, how then does the "Reason as Guide" approach to living differ from the "Reason as Master" approach, and why does he name it "anti-rationalist", but not "irrationalist"? To answer the second question first, Graham says that the anti-rationalist is a "rebel against 'Reason as Master,' the irrationalist even against 'Reason as Guide'". He then goes on to an analysis of two irrationalists—Nietzsche and de Sade—which we may pass by in order to focus on his account of the anti-rationalist who has most influenced him—Chuang-tzu. Graham situates Chuang-tzu historically as responding with skepticism to the traditional moralists of his time (the Confucians) and the utilitarian-logicians of his time (the Mohists). He also observes in justifying this exposition of Chuang-tzu that it has taken Western thought a long process of reason in detachment from spontaneity ("the great Western contribution to awareness") to reach an "impasse from which the insights of a logically less sophisticated tradition can help us retrace our steps" (*ibid.*, p. 192). Graham also suggests (here, and elsewhere) that Chuang-tzu's skepticism and hostility to rationalism in an age as deep in doubt as our own may have contributed to the subsequent direction of Chinese thought away from the commitment to logic which ancient Greece made during about the same time period (*ibid.*, p. 184).[4]

In depicting Chuang-tzu's distinctive point of view in this historical context, Graham says that while all Chinese philosophy (including Confucianism) assumed that "the springs of action are spontaneous", and that balanced action required adjustment of spontaneity to measure, the Daoists were exceptional in "directly recommending spontaneity", and, in the case of Chuang-tzu, rejecting all formulated rules of conduct, and "in denying that moralists and sophists can ever settle their differences by logical demonstration" because of the inability of language to capture what is never fixed (Graham, 1985, p. 185). Drawing upon the insights of people who really know what they are doing—cooks, meat carvers, wheelwrights, swimmers—Chuang-tzu rejects the notion that skilful action involves posing and choosing between abstractly and antecedently formulated alternatives before acting. In acting, such craftsmen reason not from first principles or even from rules they learned as apprentices. Rather, "they attend to the total situation and respond, trusting to a knack which they cannot explain in words, the hand moving of itself as the eye gazes with unflagging concentration" (*ibid.*, p. 187). On this view then, skilful action begins in spontaneity and is guided by wisdom understood not as the application of antecedently formulated rules, but as "the dispassionate mirroring of things as they objectively are":[5]

> The sage does not use the heart, the organ of thought to plan ahead, only to reflect the situation as it objectively is before he responds. Like a mirror, it reflects only the present, does not store the past experience which traps in obsolete attitudes... The metaphor of the mirror is developed in late states of *Chuang-tzu*:
> > Within yourself, no fixed positions:
> > Things as take shape disclose themselves.
> > Moving, be like water,
> > Still be like a mirror
> > Respond like an echo. (1985, p. 187)

Graham then summarizes his own involved exposition by identifying two stages in Chuang-tzu's thought, the first the articulation of the view that all principles for grounding conduct are themselves groundless; the second, a conditional skepticism that has as anchor spontaneity

---

4   See, more generally on the history of ancient Chinese thought, A.C. Graham (1989), Fung Yu-Lan (1952), and Benjamin I. Schwartz (1985).

5   Much of this is based upon the second chapter of the *Chuang-tzu*, "On the Equality of Things". I have used the translation by Victor H. Mair (1994). For Lao-tzu, I have used Hans-Georg Moeller (2007). For Leih-tzu, A.C. Graham (1960).

and its single guide, the imperative, "mirror things as they are, or 'be aware'", a purified form of concentration attained in detachment from the agitation generated by attention to the "ten thousand things" under Heaven (*ibid.*, p. 188).

At this point, having faithfully attempted a succinct summary of Graham's Daoist-based critique of Western rationalism, let us turn to Oakeshott's critique of the same as presented in several essays of *Rationalism in Politics*, before exploring how the two accounts complement one another. As I have tried to show elsewhere,[6] Oakeshott's critique of the errors of "Rationalism" in morals and politics is based on its failure to perceive the "poetic character" of human conduct and activity. Let us proceed here by watching Oakeshott develop the meaning of this phrase, and then see what it may owe to the Daoist critique of Mohist (and Confucian) rationalism as characterized by A.C. Graham. Our general intent will be to see if the meanings and implications of Oakeshott's pregnant phrase, "the poetic character of human activity" overlap with Chuang-tzu's general account of reality, and, if so, whether the meaning of some of Oakeshott's rather summarily presented ideas is enhanced by such a comparison.

Oakeshott's clearest and fullest account of a healthy and balanced morality, and of the proper role of reflective and analytic intellect within it, is to be found in the 1948 essay, "The Town of Babel" (1962, pp. 59–79). (By "morality" Oakeshott understands activity in which behaviour is determined by ideas, *implicit or explicit*, about right and wrong, good and bad.) He explicitly says that the analysis will be concerned with the form or shape of moral life, though *in practice* the form of morality is inseparable from its content. He then proposes to investigate two ideal forms of moral life, which, "either separately or in combination, compose the form of the moral life of the Western World" (*ibid.*, p. 61).

Oakeshott characterizes the first of the pure forms of moral life (which he distinguishes from any assumptions about moral intuition, moral conscience, or primitive morality) as one the form of which is a "habit of *affection and conduct*", rather than a "habit of reflective *thought*" proceeding from a choice among alternatives expressing moral ideas and rules:

> There is, on the occasion, nothing more than the unreflective following of a tradition of conduct in which we have been brought up. And such a moral habit will disclose itself as often in not doing in as in performances. (*ibid.*, p. 61)

---

6   See W.J. Coats (2000) and (2003).

Oakeshott also suggests of this first form of morality that it is the form which moral action takes (as well) in "all the emergencies of life when time and opportunity for reflection are lacking" (*ibid.*, p. 62).

Oakeshott next takes up the kind of education which generates, nurtures, and maintains this first form of moral life, suggesting that it is in an education acquired in "living with people who habitually behave in a certain manner" (*ibid.*, p. 62), an education acquired in the same way as a child acquires its native language, an education with no specifiable beginning point, and one which can be acquired without awareness of rules. (And in the case of language, if it has been acquired by the use of rules, its skilful application requires forgetting of these rules in order that speech and action not be turned into "the application of rules to a situation".) There are many things which this form of education cannot give us. We can for example learn to play a game without breaking the rules, but "we cannot acquire a knowledge of the rules themselves without in having them formulated for us... nor shall we be able to explain why the referee has blown his whistle" (*ibid.*, p. 63). Or, this kind of education can give us "the ability never to write a false line of poetry" (*ibid.*, p. 63), but not knowledge of metric forms.

In brief, this sort of moral education gives us the power to act appropriately without hesitation, but not the ability to explain our actions in terms of moral principles or abstractions. In fact, such an education may be considered a failure if it does not provide a range of behaviour sufficient "to meet all situations without the necessity of calling upon reflection, or if it does not make the habit of behaviour sufficiently compelling to remove hesitation" (*ibid.*, p. 63) in speech and action and non-action. Its virtue is to give stability to the moral life of individuals or societies, an elastic stability deriving from its resistance to systematization of its habits, so that the collapse of a part of it does not spread to other parts.

The second pure form of moral life which Oakeshott considers is one (in opposition to the first) in which activity is initiated and deter-mined by "*the reflective application of a moral criterion*". He suggests that this form of moral life itself comes in two varieties, "*the self-conscious pursuit of moral ideals*", and "*the reflective observance of moral rules*" (*ibid.*, p. 66). In this very self-conscious form of moral life, action will always be the outcome of judgments about antecedently and abstractly formu-lated moral ideals and rules, which themselves have been formulated from a belief in the importance of clear and certain principles capable of defence against criticism from other such abstract moral principles. Oakeshott notes that for this form of moral life "the situations of living" should appear ideally as "problems to be solved", problems for which "it will appear more important to have a moral ideal, than to act" (*ibid.*, pp. 66–67). Oakeshott also emphasizes the constant requirement for interpretation of ideals and rules in this form of moral life in order to translate them into behaviour, for what is important here is observance of a rule or realization of an end, "not to behave in a certain concrete manner". Tradition here is always viewed as defective and incomplete if not constantly subjected to a "corrective analysis and criticism" (*ibid.*, p. 67).

Predictably, the education required by this form of moral life will be intellectual training in managing and applying moral ideals after separating them from their "necessarily imperfect expression" in particular actions. More generally, "its aim is moral behaviour spring-ing from the communally cultivated reflective capacities of each indi-vidual" (*ibid.*, p. 67).

The strength of this form of moral education is confidence in under-standing and formulation of moral ideals and rules, but it has its dangers as well: reflection may come to inhibit genuine moral sensi-bility; there will be a constant need for moral perfection leading to eccentric attention to every moral call and, in time, an unhappy society which "in action shies and plunges like a distracted animal"; and there will be "little power of self-modification", leading, over time, to the possibility of total rejection and replacement, i.e. revolution (*ibid.*, pp. 68–69). In brief, this rationalist form of moral life always leads to chagrin and disillusionment since extreme ideals are always in tension with their opposites (justice and charity, righteousness and mercy, liberty and order, spontaneity and deliberateness, and so on). It is also a very frustrating and difficult form of moral life since verbal conflicts between moral ideals must be removed or resolved before moral behaviour is even possible. For an individual this form of moral life may have some rewards within a society not itself engaged in such a gamble — but for a society as a whole to adopt this form of moral life is a disastrous folly (*ibid.*, pp. 69–70).

Oakeshott next considers combinations of those two forms of ideal extremes (since it seems unlikely that either could exist independently), one in which the first extreme (tradition) is dominant, the other in which reflection is dominant. (Needless to say, the first mixture — sounding much like Graham's "Reason as Guide" approach — is Oakeshott's preference since it is far more likely to sustain itself, as we shall see.) In this first mixture, action (or non-action) springing from a habit of behaviour will retain its primacy over reflection, but this mixture will also enjoy the advantages of a reflective morality — "the power to criticize to reform and to explain itself", and to "spread itself through abstraction beyond its customs" (*ibid.*, pp. 69–70). Education in moral ideology will supplement education in moral habit without corrupting or disintegrating it, as in the case of a religion which has taken on a theology "without losing its character as a way of living" (*ibid.*, pp. 70–71).

By contrast, the second mixture in which the reflective extreme is dominant will have a "disintegrating affect upon a habit of behaviour" (*ibid.*, p. 71). When the self-conscious pursuit of ideals takes charge (whether in each individual or in a certain social or professional class), speculation and criticism will supervene when action is called for, and a perfectionist and intellectually and *universally* defensible moral ideology will be seen as more important than a living habit of behaviour, and if this is not available then there will be silence and inaction (not because this is an appropriate response, but by default). The most radical defect of this mixture of moral life is its denial of "*the poetic character of all human activity*" (*ibid.*, p. 72), Oakeshott's summary phrase for a view of human experience, especially evident in artistic and moral life, in which the form and content of thought and action arise simultaneously:

> What the poet says and what he wants to say are not two things... he does not know what he wants to say until he has said it... And what is true of poetry is true also... of all human moral activity... *Moral ideas* are not, in the first place, the products of reflective thought... *They are the products of human behaviour... to which reflective thought gives subsequent, partial and abstract expression in words.* (*ibid.*, pp. 72–73, emphasis added)

Oakeshott then spends the remainder of the essay showing how it came about from both Greco-Roman and early Christian sources, that modern European morality, since the seventeenth century especially, has been a mixture in which the pursuit of moral ideals has been dominant, to its detriment:

> Self-consciousness is asked to be creative, and habit is given the role of critic; what should be subordinate has come to rule, and its rule is mis-rule. (*ibid.*, p. 75)

Before attempting to gather up and compare what we have gleaned thus far from Graham and Oakeshott, let us look first, very summarily, at Oakeshott's analysis of the errors of Rationalism in three other essays — "Rationalism in Politics", "Rational Conduct", and "Political Education". In this first essay, Oakeshott criticizes "Rationalism" (citing the story from *Chuang-tzu* of Duke Han and the wheelwright) for its failure to recognize two kinds of inseparable knowledge in any concrete activity — technical knowledge which can be formulated in words and put in books, and practical knowledge of timing and judgment which cannot, and is passed on only in an apprenticeship. Out of a misplaced desire for certainty, the Rationalist focuses on techniques with identifiable starting and ending points, in the mistaken belief that technique is self-contained and contains the practical knowledge for its own skilful application (*ibid.*, pp. 7–13).

In the essay "Rational Conduct", Oakeshott traces this mistaken belief in the sovereignty and universality of technique to a mistaken conception of mind as a neutral apparatus for thinking, detached from its historically acquired subject matters; but for Oakeshott mind is its historically acquired beliefs and ideas about how to behave appropriately in specific circumstances, and cannot exist in advance of conduct (*ibid.*, p. 90). It is the result of reflection on conduct, understood as desirous human energy being active in a certain way: "no activity is rational outside of the particular idiom to which it belongs" (*ibid.*, p. 102):[7] what makes action "rational", carefully speaking, is its place in a "flow of sympathy, a current of moral action":

> An impulsive action, a "spontaneous outburst," activity in obedience to a custom or to a rule, and an action... preceded by a long reflective process may, alike, be "rational"... What establishes harmony... is the concrete mind, a mind composed wholly of activities in search of harmony ... (1962, p. 109)

In the third such essay, "Political Education", Oakeshott develops the idea of the "pursuit of intimations" as an alternative to the Rationalist application of political ideologies and moral codes. This phrase is used to indicate the idea that formal political and legal change should follow, rather than initiate, what people are already doing in practice. To pursue "intimations" in political life, then, is to formalize or legalize those practices which, over time, have shown themselves to fit harmoniously in a comprehensive, concrete way of life (*ibid.*, p. 129, pp. 133–136).

Now, the aim in making this comparative exploration has been to illustrate the claim that Oakeshott's critique of "Rationalism" is enhanced and enriched by seeing what it owes to, and where it differs from, certain ideas of the *Chuang-tzu* as interpreted by A.C. Graham. In particular, it has meant to show, from a different angle, the ramifications of what is arguably the central idea from which many of

---

7   See also in this context Roger T. Ames (1998), p. 220—"Situation has primacy, and agency is an abstraction from it"—and p. 226—"...the notion of discrete human agency in the Western tradition derives arguably from an historical analogy between the human beings' essential self... and Diety. The essentializing copula verb ('is...') establishes the static agent... By contrast... the classical Chinese language has no copula verb that would entail separation of agent from action...". On the danger of projecting a modern conception of "self" onto the pluralistic personhood presumed in the *Chuang-tzu*, see Chris Joachim (1998).

Oakeshott's other ideas flow—the idea of the "poetic character" of human activity and conduct. As I have tried to show elsewhere,[8] this is a claim about the structure of all experiential reality, evident (before he was using the phrase or had developed his ideas on artistic experience) as far back as *Experience and Its Modes* (1933). The central idea here is that the structure of human, experiential reality is not *prosaic*—rather it is *poetic* or creative in the sense that its form and content, *how* it knows and does and *what* it knows and does, arise simultaneously and fluidly, neither in advance of the other, and that, by implication, balanced, skilful activity will mirror this existential and experiential structure, rather than resist or deny it. This is the basis for Oakeshott's critique of even ancient (Platonic) rationalism for its blindness in formulating imperatives about copying antecedently crafted forms and models (1962, pp. 219–220, 224 note 1).

The specific question to be pursued then is the overlap or coincidence between Oakeshott's comprehensive idea about the poetic character of human conduct and activity and Graham's account of Taoist-like spontaneity (things that are so "of themselves").[9] To rehearse, the "spontaneous" for Graham refers to that which is not the result of considered choice; his general argument, that all conscious choices of ends and means are dependent on non-reflective or spontaneous pulls, to which analytic reason (in its best relation) serves as critical guide.[10] And, again, Graham is careful to distinguish this view from the Romantic idealization of Nature or the surrealist surrender to automatism[11]—spontaneity is not desirable as and end in itself or as the

---

[8] See note #6, above.

[9] Graham translates the Chinese *tzǔ-jen* (literally, "being so of itself") as "spontaneity" to describe human accord with the Way or Tao, understood as inhuman processes of heaven and earth which are themselves indifferent to individual human beings. If a man wishes to return to the Way, he must "discard knowledge... refuse to impose... his principles on nature, recover the spontaneity of the newborn child, allow his actions to be 'so of themselves' like physical processes... Perfectly concentrated and perfectly relaxed, like... the charioteer whose hand reacts immediately to the give and pull of... the reins..." (Graham, 1960, pp. 2–3).

[10] For a related view (in addition to Oakeshott) from a Western philosopher of science, see Alfred North Whitehead (1929), who argues that the biological function of reason is to rescue the human creative impulse from chaos and anarchy.

[11] For the view that the intuitions of surrealists such as André Breton were close to the visions of the *Chuang-tzu* and offer an escape from Cartesian mind–body dualism, see Jean Francois Billeter (2002, p. 167): "Je pense aux surréalistes... Queleques unes de leur intuitions... les placent dans le voisinage du *Tchouang-tseu*." Obviously, the surrealist emphasis on non-

source of all value. It (like analytic reason) is itself to be evaluated by its capacity to contribute to enhanced (expanded and intensified) awareness of self and situation, evident in appropriate action in any particular instance. Increased awareness, in turn, is seen as a progression toward things done for their own sake, until reaching a terminus in artistic or aesthetic experience, experience had solely for its own sake.[12] Although Graham's account of artistic experience as emblematic of the highest state of awareness differs from Oakeshott's in drawing practical ramifications, these are, in fact, similarities in their respective accounts of artistic or poetic experience which are worth exploring here for the light they shed on the moral and practical implications of Oakeshott's central idea about the "poetic character of human activity", implications which he himself did not often care to indicate.

The brunt of Graham's account of aesthetic experience is to show that many of the traditional explanations of art and artistic experience of both the artist and the spectator (such as unity within variety, the beauty of the whole, unity of form and content) can be seen as expressions of greater awareness; that works of art are to be seen as captured, public expressions of "aware spontaneity". The way in which art affects especially the spectator or reader is, in fact, to "break down the habit of noticing only the practically relevant, *and restore the plenitude of the response when the senses are open to what normally eludes them*" (1985, p. 89).[13] (Thus, although Graham's aim is ultimately practical—heightened awareness—this is achieved by transcending the narrowly practical.) And it is the spontaneous restoration of plenitude or fullness of response which contributes to heightened awareness of self and situation. For Graham this is also a moral awareness:

> On the argument of this book, to think morally, is to synthesize one's reactions from the viewpoint of all involved. If so, when the subject of a

---

logical and dream-like techniques to bridge from unconscious to conscious mind has affinities to Daoist attempts to escape the contradictions of the phenomenal world through spontaneous submission to, and channelling of, the Dao. For Graham, however, surrealism remains a form of irrationalism (vs. anti-rationalism) which places intensity of experience before self and situational awareness.

12   "But for an ethic derived from 'Be aware' its supreme function will be to evoke a response justified as an end in itself by its heightening of awareness... The works most highly valued for themselves are commonly dignified by the name of 'Art'..." (1985, p. 67).

13   Contrast Oakeshott here: "Nor are these difficulties avoided in the more modest claim that poetic imaging is seeing 'things' as they are when perception is unclouded by preoccupations of desire, approval, curiosity or inquiry" (1962, p. 230).

work of art is human relations, there will be no difference between being aesthetically successful and being moral. (*ibid.*, p. 70)

By contrast, Oakeshott denies the thought that poetic or artistic experience be evaluated or understood in terms of practical and moral aims or that it has access to any superior reality or truth (although even Oakeshott cannot deny that poetic experience may have practical and moral effects which someone else may care to trace).[14] On Oakeshott's account, poetic experience is intermittent moments of contemplative imaging and delight (for both creator and observer) achieved in the unity of form and content, of a *how* and *what* of expression, both of which arise simultaneously:

> A poet does not do three things: first experience... an emotion, then contemplate it, and finally seeks a means of expressing the results of his contemplation; he does one thing only, he imagines poetically.
> ...a poetic utterance (a work of art) is not the expression of an experience, it is the experience and the only one there is. (1962, p. 232)

Nevertheless, in spite of Oakeshott's attempt to isolate poetic (artistic) experience from all practical and scientific and philosophic concerns, he bases his account of the structure of experiential reality and his critique of Rationalism's implicit denial of this structure upon the "poetic character of all human activity".[15] One might go so far as to say in this context that both Oakeshott and Graham's *Chuang-tzu* base a critique of the errors of prosaic Rationalism upon an affirmation of the aesthetic or poetic structure of experiential reality, in which, as we have seen, aware or appropriate action is never the result of reflective choice among antecedently conceived models or alternatives. And in this context, I believe it is possible to make the case that Oakeshott's critique of the errors of Rationalism is that they are in fact moral errors, properly understood, or have deleterious moral effects, to be more precise. If this is in fact the case, then comparisons such as this with Graham's *Chuang-tzu* may qualify criticisms made of Oakeshott as being unconcerned with moral considerations in politics.[16]

In his late, theoretical work, Oakeshott defines a moral practice (by its high level of generality) as a practice with "no extrinsic purpose"

---

14 Even Oakeshott concedes that appreciation of the voice of poetry or art in the human conversation may afford some relief from the monotony of its recent domination by the voices of science and practice (1962, p. 203).

15 See note #6 above, and Oakeshott (1933), and the long essay, "The Voice of Poetry in the Conversation of Mankind", in *Rationalism in Politics* (pp. 197–247).

16 See, for example, David Walsh (1997, pp. 56–65) and Paul Franco (1999, pp. 247–248). I do not, however, mean to imply by this that Oakeshott's ultimate concerns are moral or practical ones.

(1975, p. 62), and distinguishes it from an instrumental practice with aims capable of unambiguous achievement in substantive utterance and action. Implicit in Oakeshott's definition of a moral practice as one with no extrinsic purpose (similar to Graham's definition of aesthetic experience) is recognition in it of the role played by what Oakeshott earlier called practical (or traditional) knowledge, distinguished from the technical knowledge which can be formulated in words and rules, and put in books. Practical knowledge, we may recall, was that part of knowledge of how to do something concerned with its more general and elusive aspects, such as a sense of timing and propriety, as well as a sense of when not to act or speak at all. Arguably, Oakeshott's critique of modern Rationalism, for its reduction of knowledge (in both theory and practice) to technical, propositional knowledge, amounts to a charge of moral error as well, in making moral practices negligible or peripheral, and displacing them as an important source of both skill and human meaning in the life of any civilization which adopts and institutionalizes the Rationalist perspective (and without offering anything to take the place of practical knowledge). All of this follows from Rationalism's denial of the very existence of practical or traditional knowledge about how to act skilfully and appropriately on account of its occurring at such a general level as to lack extrinsic, substantive purposes (even though following a morality may residually accomplish these as well). Thus, it may not be an exaggeration to say that Oakeshott's implicit claim is that Rationalism in politics and social and religious life makes a moral life, carefully speaking, impossible, as well as closing off entirely an important source of human meaning.[17] Or at a minimum, as our summary of "The Tower of Babel" indicated, it makes a balanced moral and political life (where reflective and analytic reason play a secondary, critical role) impossible, and generates self-perpetuating incoherence in the lives of civilizations which adopt or evolve into a comprehensive Rationalist perspective.

Rather than simply rehearse (by way of summary) the points of similarity in Graham's account of spontaneity and Oakeshott's account of the poetic character of human activity, let us look more generally at what Oakeshott's view shares with all ancient Chinese Taoist thought. Graham argues in another work that in spite of differences among the *Lao-tzu*, *Chuang-tzu*, and *Leih-tzu*, all "share one basic insight, that while other things move spontaneously on the course proper to them, man

---

17   For a similar view (based on an argument about Oakeshott's place in the Idealist self-realization tradition), see Stuart Isaacs (2006). In my view, Isaacs goes too far in attempting to fit Oakeshott comprehensively in this tradition.

has separated himself from the Way (Tao) by reflecting, posing alternatives, and formulating principles of action" (1989, p. 172).[18] By implication, then, the aim of contented and skilful living is to find its way back to "the Way", understood as some sort of whole, transcendent or not, which is allowed to act through one. And for Graham's *Chuang-tzu*, as we have seen, this includes the use of "Reason as Guide" rather than "Reason as master".

Now, what does Oakeshott share with this perspective? He clearly shares its moderate skepticism toward the limited capacity of conscious intellect to grasp (and control) reality with certainty, or to express it in propositions made up of words, evident in his choice of the essay form of writing, and heavy reliance on rhetorical tropes such as hyperbole, and on metaphor and understanding by analogy. He also shares its appreciation of the importance of practical skill as the most important analogue for moral and political life. His idea of the "pursuit of intimations" in politics and moral life as the basis for formal change reflects a belief in the importance of putting oneself in touch with some sort of harmonious whole (similar to the Tao, even if expressed in Hegelian[19] and Bradlean terms), as well as a recognition that adopting an holistic perspective is an intelligent way of transcending the disputations between dyadic opposites such as "liberty and order" and "righteousness and mercy". And, most saliently, Oakeshott's idea of the poetic character of human activity actually refines or develops the

---

18 Graham, p. 172. For the unusual view that it is a mistake even to classify Chuang-tzu as a Daoist thinker owing to his Confucian influences and his differences with Lao-tzu over the source of reality, see Belleter (2002, pp. 135–137). In this discussion, Belleter is also critical of the general Western practice of using the term Daoism to refer to what Chinese intellectual culture would separate into four or five separate traditions. Belleter's strongest methodological point here, in my view, is that we be alert to the confusion which results from applying the epithet "Daoist" to a source, and then imputing various "Daoist" ideas to a thinker in lieu of reading a text for what it actually says or implies. Nevertheless, and *malgré tout*, I think Graham's general point (about this common thread in all "Daoist" thought) will stand. For more on a common theme in both Lao-tzŭ and Chuang-tzu, see Schwartz (1985, pp. 216–219). For the view that the unifying theme of the composite *Chuang-tzu* is a teaching about overcoming obstructions (such as rule-oriented techniques, egoism, desire for reputation, appetites) to "one's carefree flowing with the world of living things", see Joachim (1998, p. 36).

19 According to Oakeshott biographer Robert Grant (in private correspondence), Oakeshott read and discussed Emile Haveloque's 1923 book, *China*, which is keen on the similarity between the Daoist and Hegelian impulses to transcend the oppositions and contradictions of phenomenal life. See Emile Haveloque (1923, pp. 127–144).

Daoist imperative for aware spontaneity, by grounding a critique of Rationalism upon an expansively articulated account of the poetic or creative structure of all human experiential reality.

To conclude this exploration on a note of difference, Oakeshott's account of the poetic or creative character of human activity does provide a nuance not evident in contemporary secondary accounts of spontaneity and submission in the Dao, in the following regard. Roger Ames, for example, has argued characteristically that the account of God as the unchanging and perfect primary causal agent in the Judeo-Christian tradition is the source of the Western paradigm of the autonomous and detached moral agent (made in His image) who shapes his/her life and the world to purposive designs. All of this is contrasted with the classical Chinese commitment to a mutable, moving, developmental process which assumes no separation of essence and attribute, and no abstracted agent, but rather a person understood as "the compounding narrative of what one does — an always unique field of experiences, beliefs, and feelings" (Ames, 1998, p. 226).

Now, Oakeshott, in my view, would fall between the cracks of Ames' two, stark alternatives, in drawing upon the distinction (within the Western philosophic and theological tradition) between a *created* being or thing and a *crafted* being or thing. The critical distinction here in Western philosophy and theology[20] is that in a created being or thing existence is not accidental to essence, but adds to it (as in Anselm's well known "ontological proof" for the existence of God). This idea also implies that a created being or thing has no *telos* or purpose known independently or in advance of its historical unfolding. While Ames' characterization of the Western view would fit the account of the Demiurge in Plato's *Timaeus*, a divine craftsman informing matter with pre-existing forms and purposes, his account will not easily fit the Augustinian account of creation *ex nihilo*, or that part of the medieval Christian tradition less influenced by Aquinas and Aristotle.

In my view, and as other essays in this collection make clearer, Oakeshott has managed to draw artfully upon this Western "creative" tradition to incorporate in his mid-twentieth-century writings certain Daoist ideas about the unreflective springs of skill and morality, without making them seem alien and exotic (in a fashion similar to Cicero's accounts for Roman audiences of Greek philosophic and ethical ideas). Oakeshott approximates the Daoist "situational self" by polishing up

---

[20]   The fullest account known to me of the implications of the differences between creation and craft (*techne*) is to be found in M.B. Foster (1935), which is critical of both thinkers in its title for failure to grasp these differences. See, also, M.B. Foster (1934, pp. 446–468).

the unreflective side of morality as a tradition of behaviour; by critiquing the Cartesian view of the mind as a neutral instrument detachable from its historically acquired experiences; and by treating the border between "self" and "non-self" as variable depending upon the particular way of being active at the moment.[21]

References

Ames, R. (ed.) (1998) *Wandering at Ease in the Zhuangzi*, pp. 220, 226, Albany, NY: State University of New York Press.

Billeter, J.F. (2002) *Leçons sur tchouang-tseu*, pp. 135–137, Paris: Editions Allia.

Botwinik, A. (2011) *Michael Oakeshott's Skepticism*, p. 140, Princeton, NJ: Princeton University Press.

Coats, W.J. (2000) *Oakeshott and His Contemporaries*, pp. 103–109, London: Associated University Presses.

Coats, W.J. (2003) *Political Theory and Practice*, pp. 101–111, London: Associated University Presses.

Foster, M.B. (1934) "The Christian Doctrine of Creation and the Rise of Modern Natural Science", *Mind*, Vol. 43, 173.

Foster, M.B. (1935) *The Political Philosophies of Plato and Hegel*, Oxford: Oxford University Press.

Franco, P. (1999) *Hegel's Philosophy of Freedom*, pp. 247–248, New Haven, CT: Yale University Press.

Fung Yu-han (1952) *A History of Chinese Philosophy*, Bodde, D. (trans.), Princeton, NJ: Princeton University Press.

Graham, A.C. (1960) *The Book of Leih-tzu*, London: John Murray.

Graham, A.C. (1989) *Disputers of the Tao*, La Salle, AL: Open Court.

Haveloque, E. (1923) *China*, London: J.M. Dent.

Isaacs, S. (2006) *The Politics and Philosophy of Michael Oakeshott*, New York: Routledge.

Joachim, C. (1998) "Just Say No to 'No Self' in Zhuangzi", in Ames, R. (1998), p. 36, pp. 37–74.

Mair, V. (1994) *Wandering in the Way: Early Taoist Tales and Parables of Chuang-tzu*, Honolulu, HI: University of Hawaii Press.

Moeller, H.-G. (2007) *Daodejiug: A Complete Translation and Commentary*, Chicago, IL: Open Court.

---

[21] Oakeshott (1962, p. 204): "The self appears as activity... There is nothing antecedent to it... Further, on every occasion this activity is a specific mode of activity..." See also, in this connection, Aryeh Botwinick (2011, p. 140): "The optimal self for Oakeshott is one *characterized by a reduced self-consciousness that allows for the play of different impulses* and an ongoing process of self-discovery" (emphasis added).

Oakeshott, M.J. (1975) *On Human Conduct,* Oxford: Oxford University Press.

Oakeshott, M.J. (1962) *Rationalism in Politics and Other Essays,* London: Methuen and Co.

Schwitzgebel, E. (1996) "Zhuangzi's Attitude Toward Language and His Skepticism", in Khellberg, P. & Ivanhoe, P. (eds.) *Essays on Skepticism, Relativism and Ethics in the Zhuanzi,* pp. 86–88, Albany, NY: State University of New York.

Schwartz, B. (1985) *The World of Thought in Ancient China,* Cambridge, MA: Harvard University Press.

Walsh, D. (1997) *The Growth of the Liberal Soul,* Columbia, MO: University of Missouri Press.

Whitehead, A.N. (1929) *The Function of Reason,* Princeton, NJ: Princeton University Press.

Four

Oakeshott's Descartes, Vico's Descartes

In his well-known 1947 essay "Rationalism in Politics", Michael Oakeshott traced the intellectual seeds of modern Rationalism in politics and morals (a belief in the sovereignty of technique) to René Descartes and Francis Bacon, or at least to their disciples:

> By a pardonable abridgement of history, the Rationalist character may be seen springing from the exaggeration of Bacon's hopes and the neglect of the skepticism of Descartes... Descartes never becomes a Cartesian, but as Bouillier says of the seventeenth century, "le cartesianisme a triomphé... non seulement dans la philosophie, mais les sciences et les lettres ellesmemes..." (1962, p. 17)

Oakeshott doesn't say very much about Descartes (or Bacon) in this essay, but he does draw upon their thought in expounding the basic outlook of what he calls "modern Rationalism". In this essay I propose to summarize Oakeshott's account and critique of those of Descartes' (and Bacon's) ideas which led to Rationalism as the dominant political and moral outlook in European civilization of the past four centuries, and then compare that brief account with the criticisms of Descartes and Cartesianism by the eighteenth-century Neopolitan thinker (and professor of rhetoric) Gambattista Vico. By looking at Vico's spirited (but different) critique of Cartesianism, as well as bringing in Descartes' own arguments where relevant, I hope to make an informed assessment of the justness of Oakeshott's characterization of Descartes' influence in the outlook of what he calls "modern Rationalism".

Oakeshott begins his essay with a character sketch of "the Rationalist":

> ...[H]e stands (he always *stands*) for independence of mind on all occasions, for thought free from obligation to any authority save the authority of "reason"... he is the *enemy* of authority, of prejudice, of the merely traditional, customary or habitual... (*ibid.*, p. 1)

After also characterizing the Rationalist political style—a problem-solving approach for perfect solutions universally applicable—Oakeshott goes on to search for the deeper springs of the Rationalist orientation, "a doctrine about human knowledge" (*ibid.*, p. 7). In order to explain his view of Rationalism's doctrine about knowledge, Oakeshott distinguishes two kinds of inseparable (except in analysis) knowledge in all skilful activity (including science and art), technical knowledge and practical knowledge, and then suggests that Rationalism is a denial that the latter is knowledge at all (*ibid.*, p. 4). *Technical knowledge* or knowledge of technique for Oakeshott is that part of a skill which can formulated in rules, and deliberately learned, retained, and applied; in brief, that part of a skill which may be precisely formulated and put between the covers of a book (e.g. a cook book). *Practical knowledge* for Oakeshott is that part of a skill which exists only in use, cannot be formulated in rules, involves matters of judgment, imagination, and timing, and can be acquired only through an apprenticeship in contact with one who knows how to practice it; and this is as true for the experimental scientist as for the craftsman.

Oakeshott's understanding is that Rationalism is the assertion that the only element of knowledge in activity is technical knowledge: "The sovereignty of 'reason', for the Rationalist, means the sovereignty of technique" (*ibid.*, p. 11). Oakeshott suggests that the Rationalist preoccupation with techniques derives from a preoccupation with certainty, and techniques do *seem* or appear to provide the certainty which comes with a self-contained system of identifiable starting and ending points, between which techniques can be mechanistically applied with no required additional knowledge. For Oakeshott, of course, all of this is the Rationalist illusion—both the claim of certainty and the appearance of self-completeness:

> As with every other sort of knowledge, learning a technique does not consist of getting rid of pure ignorance, but in reforming knowledge which is already there. Nothing, not even the most nearly self-contained technique (the rules of a game) can in fact be imparted to an empty mind; and what is imparted is nourished by what is already there. (*ibid.*, p. 12)

Oakeshott next turns to the provenance of this dominant post-Renaissance European intellectual fashion, and it is here that he characterizes and discusses the influence of Bacon and Descartes. Although Oakeshott concedes that Descartes does more of his own skepticism than Bacon,[1] he characterizes both as making explicit slowly mediated changes of several centuries in the demand for a self-contained, certain, precisely formulated technique of inquiry, which can only begin in an emptied mind ("the technique of research begins with an intellectual purge"[2]), and which is ideally characterized by a mechanical-like and universal application.[3] And Oakeshott also makes clear his own sympathies with Pascal's critique of Descartes on the point of certain knowledge, namely that probable knowledge is more certain than "certain" knowledge:

> Descartes must begin with something so sure that it cannot be doubted, and was led, as a consequence, to believe that all genuine knowledge is technical knowledge. Pascal avoided this conclusion by his doctrine of probability—the paradox that probable knowledge has more of the whole truth than certain knowledge. Secondly, Pascal perceived that the human mind... is not wholly dependent for its success upon a conscious formulated technique... The precise formulation of rules of inquiry endangers the success of inquiry by exaggerating the importance of method... (1962, p. 20)

Before turning to Descartes' own writings on method of inquiry in an attempt to ascertain the accuracy of Oakeshott's characterizations of it, let us look at Vico's eighteenth-century critique of Descartes' method, and Cartesianism, generally.

Vico's critique is much more historical and psychological than Oakeshott's and is part of a comprehensive philosophy of mind, based on the ideas of recollective imagination and recollective universals, and which Donald Verene claims is highly original, and to be distinguished from all forms of rationalism, idealism, and empiricism (1981, p. 31). I shall bring in only as much of Vico's mature, comprehensive philosophy as is necessary for a grasp of his criticism of Cartesian philosophy. And I bring Vico's critique of Descartes into the analysis because his general conclusions (about the disastrous practical effects upon balanced and skilful human activity generated by the ubiquitous introduction of clear and certain universal methods) are similar to Oakeshott's, but are reached from very different analytic points of departure. Hence, they not only shed light on Oakeshott's abbreviated critique of Descartes, but provide more specific criticisms for

---

[1] Recognizing in chapter six of the *Discourse de la Methode* that it is "an error to suppose that the method can ever be the sole means of inquiry" (1962, p. 17).

[2] "The first principle of Descartes is 'de ne recevoi jamais aucune chose pour vraie que je ne le connusse évidemment être telle...'" (Oakeshott, 1962, p. 16).

[3] Oakeshott quotes Bacon from the *Novum Organum* on the new method which "places all wits and understandings nearly on a level" (1962, p. 15).

evaluation when we come to Descartes' own writing (and that of later Cartesians). By way of a bridge from Oakeshott's critique of Descartes to Vico's, I simply note that what Vico provides in *On the Study Methods of Our Time, On the Most Ancient Wisdom of the Italians,* and in the *New Science,* is an account of mind and its development which may be viewed as a very detailed "fleshing out" of what Oakeshott calls simply practical (versus technical) knowledge, i.e. knowledge which is acquired in apprenticeship and cannot be reduced to rule-stipulated methods.

Vico's criticism of the extension of Cartesian mathematical analytic method into the realm of pedagogy, morals, and law derives from his belief (based on detailed historical research into the etymology of words) in a natural or "psychogenetic"[4] order of development in both individuals and civilizations, which begins in poetic and symbolic imagination and only *culminates* in critical analytic thinking; thus, one of Vico's salient fears is pedagogical—that the near-ubiquitous intro-duction of Descartes' four-step process of understanding (based on the critical refinement, division, and categorization of sure and certain starting points) into the education of the young will dry up, so to speak, the springs of the mind, springs which generate techniques such as Descartes' method. Instead, the education of youth should be devoted to nourishing memory, imagination, and creative or inventive thinking through immersion in the kinds of rhetorical and humanistic studies Descartes himself received but then rejects for others. In addition, Vico (reminiscent here of Plato's *Republic*) fears that the methods of scientific criticism (if they are given exclusively, and too soon) will be destructive of common sense, a sense based on perception of what is only probable (not certain), the area between truth and falsity where most of human life and speech occurs:

> Philosophical criticism is the subject which we compel our youths to take up first. Now such speculative criticism… places upon the… plane of falsity… those secondary verities and ideas which are based upon probability alone and commands us to clear our minds of them. Such an approach is distinctly harmful, since training in common sense is essential to be the education of adolescents… I may add that common sense, besides being the criterion of practical judgment, is also the guiding standard of eloquence… (Vico, 1990, p. 13)

This concern about correct pedagogical order in the cultivation of inventive minds is also the basis for Vico's fear of the introduction of

---

4   For a lucid characterization of Vico's "psychogenetic" order of develop-ment, see Elio Gianturcos's introduction to Giambattista Vico (1990, p. xxxix).

analytic, algebraic Cartesian geometry in lieu of linear, synthetic, figurative geometry:

> Youth's natural inclination to the arts in which imagination or memory… is prevalent (such as painting, poetry, oratory, jurisprudence) should by no mean be blunted. Nor should advanced philosophical criticism… be an impediment to any of them. The Ancients knew how to avoid this drawback… the role of logic was fulfilled by geometry. *Following… the bent of Nature, the Ancients required their youth to learn the science of geometry which cannot be grasped without a vivid capacity to form images…* (ibid., p. 14, emphasis added)

Since Cartesian geometry gives algebraic formulations for the equivalent of geometric shapes, it did not nourish (but dried up on Vico's view) the mind's capacity to form images, a capacity which along with memory and eloquence (the learned ability to see and express connections among ostensibly disparate phenomena) gives the human mind its distinctive force.

Yet Vico's criticism of Cartesianism, especially in later works like the *New Science*, does not stop at pedagogy. Vico is concerned about the tendency of all philosophy, but especially modern skeptical philosophy, to undermine religion and authority, and hence civil order. Mark Lilla, in his book *G.B. Vico: The Making of an Anti-Modern*, has drawn out Vico's teaching on the role of ancient Roman common sense (understood as an unreflective attachment to religion, authority, marriage, and property) in the historic achievement of civilization and civil order, an achievement undermined especially by Cartesian doubt and "purge" of mind:

> The fault appears to lie in the very nature of philosophic reflection, which applies the rule of reason to less than reasonable human activities. It first sets itself against poetry, the eloquent language in which wisdom must initially be experienced… *Philosophy then fails to distinguish between the results of rational metaphysics* and mathematics, on the one hand, *and the more probabalistic rules by which the city must be governed*, on the other. It soon loosens itself from all reins of prudent wisdom and tries to apply its reason directly to politics, producing inflexible ideas… (Lilla, 1993, pp. 211–212)

Hence, for Vico, the great danger in the Cartesian purge is that it begins by trying to empty the mind of the indistinct customs and vague ideas which are the basis of what accumulated human wisdom there is. Here is Vico himself (in the *New Science*) on this point:

> This divine architect has sent forth the world of nations with vulgar wisdom as its rule. Vulgar wisdom is a common sense possessed by each people… which regulates our social lives… (in Lilla, 1993, p. 158)

Thus, the central Vichian critique of Descartes' method (especially when extended to all subjects at all pedagogic stages) is similar to Oakeshott's—it cannot account for its own activity. But in Vico's case, we are also given a theory of the historical development of the human mind in the context of historically achieved practices and customs, and an account of the proper pedagogy for developing this historically evolved mind, i.e. a pedagogy which only brings in Cartesian critical analysis after the proper formation of the imaginative and recollective faculties:

> *It is perhaps this studied ignorance of the imagination that most seriously undermines the new critical method, preventing it from achieving even its own aims.* For all criticism, Vico contends, depends first on the ability to imagine the alternatives to be analyzed. The ancients taught this imaginative skill through a highly developed art... the discipline of "topics." This art taught the discovery of appropriate arguments in matters only allowing of probable and uncertain evidence and was conceived as a preparation for... the art of analysis... The Cartesians disdained all intercourse with the undemonstrable, ignoring that practical wisdom which 'seeks out truth as it is...' (*ibid.*, p. 49, emphasis added)

Having summarized the Oakeshottian and Vichian charges against the method of Descartes and the Cartesians, let us turn to Descartes' own writings in an attempt to assess the force and accuracy of these criticisms. Since I think the case is so clear-cut, rather than create a false drama of inquiry in which the reader is asked to await the sifting of evidence for a judgment on this question, I'll simply offer mine and try to explain my reasoning. Based on a re-reading of the *Discourse on the Method*, the *Regulae*, and the *Meditations*, as well as on some older[5] and newer[6] secondary literature, it is clear to me at least that neither Oakeshott nor Vico overstates the intent and effect of Descartes' entire project. (If anything, both understate the case by exempting Descartes himself from the epithet "Cartesian".) In my view, the epithet "Cartesian" does apply to Descartes for the following reasons. First, it is clear that Descartes envisioned an explicit project which would displace in influence a scholastic philosophy based on Aristotelian doctrines about different methods of inquiry for different subject matters, and about theoretical and metaphysical observation based on sense experience. Descartes clearly strove for the establishment of a universal and certain method of inquiry, applicable to all subject matters, including the conduct of life. Secondly, in my view it is clear

---

5   Especially, A. Boyce Gibson (1967).
6   Especially, Stephen Menn (1993) *Descartes and Augustine* (Cambridge: Cambridge University Press).

that Descartes also thought seriously about how to change minds on a large scale in order to marshal societal resources behind the applications of his new method in various fields of endeavour (especially medicine) for the relief and advancement of the human species. Such considerations require that his arguments be assessed from the standpoint of rhetorical and political perspectives as well. Finally, I believe it is also clear that Descartes' "method" cannot account for his own philosophizing (as Oakshott and Vico maintain), as is apparent in the often syllogistical and probable reasoning in *The Meditations*. In support of these claims, let us turn to Descartes' own writing and to select secondary literature on that writing.

Regarding Descartes' overall project, one can turn either to his own words in the autobiographical *Discourse* or to secondary literature placing him in historical context. Let us do both. Here is Descartes on his own aims in perfecting the "natural light" of reason in himself through the steps of his own method:

> As soon, however, as I had acquired some general notions regarding physics and… had observed how far… they differ from the principles hitherto employed, I believed that I could not keep them hidden without grievously sinning against the law which lays us *under obligation to promote… the general good of mankind*. For they led me to see that it is possible to obtain knowledge highly useful in life, and *in place of the speculative philosophy taught in the Schools, we can have* a *practical philosophy*, by means of which, knowing the force and the action of fire, water, air, of the stars, of the heavens… we may employ them in all the uses for which they are suited, *thus rendering ourselves the masters and possessors of nature*. (Smith, 1952, p. 151, emphasis added)

In a seventy-odd page introduction to his book on Descartes and Augustine placing Descartes in the context of the philosophical and theological debates of the seventeenth century, Stephen Menn fleshes out these aims in great detail. Menn documents, among other aims, that Descartes was interested in providing, and encouraged to provide, an alternative to the scholastic Aristotelian philosophy which would ground metaphysics and physics in something more certain than sense-experience and less circular than scholastic definitions and syllogisms; and ground the conduct of life in deduction from "first principles", rather than in the practical wisdom of the Aristotelians, or of humanists like Montaigne. Menn also shows that Descartes' own way of thinking about the conduct of life and about political and moral matters was highly "rationalist", envisioning the application to life of the first principles derived from the methical investigation of nature, and disdaining historically evolved (rather than planned) cities as well as common law legal systems such as that of the English. Here are some of Menn's observations in these regards:

> *Descartes was genuinely concerned to make his metaphysics self-justifying and* *independent of any doctrine of the physical world*; this was necessary if the metaphysics was to be strong enough to support a complete philosophy, and... physics, without the risk of circularity. It is nonetheless clear that Descartes took the central concepts of his metaphysics from Augustine or Augustinians; if he altered... this metaphysics in the process, this was because of the constraints imposed by his project of making it the foundation of a mechanical physics. (Menn, 1993, pp 15–16, emphasis added)

> In the notes called *Cogitationes Privatae... Descartes declares that "the* *sayings of the sages can be reduced to some few general rules"*: once we master the rules... the Stoic praise of virtue will appear... as the straightforward application of our natural knowledge to the conduct of life. (*ibid.*, p. 31, emphasis added)

> Descartes draws similar inferences from legislation: *it is better for the laws* *of a city to be decreed by a single legislator...* than to evolve over time like the common laws of England... Only the former are genuinely the work of reason... *a framework for human activity can be effective only if it is created* *by some one person with a master rational plan*, and not simply through an accretion of reactions to circumstances... But the sciences, and our opinions generally, are just such accretions... (*ibid.*, p. 33, emphasis added)

In my view, it is clear and non-controversial that Descartes had a life-long project to try, as prudently as possible, to *replace* scholastic and Aristotelian metaphysics, physics, ethics, and rhetoric with a new philosophy based on a unified and universally applicable method grounded in algebra and analytic geometry, and calculated to provide (in the way it selected and organized information[7]) for the incremental "possession and mastery of nature" by the human species. Descartes' Rationalism had roots in older rationalisms of Plato and Plotinus as mediated by Augustine, especially the insight that we could be more certain about the realm of intelligibles than the realm of bodies; but it also had roots in Hebraic teachings about a wilfully *created* universe[8] and in Christian teachings about the capacity of wilfully directed intro-spection to penetrate cyclical pagan ideas about the cosmos and nature, and attain partial insight into the true God and the created universe.[9]

---

7   For some interesting observations on the connections between the nomol-ogical sciences and technology, see Jurgen Habermas (1968).

8   See, in this connection, M.B. Foster (1934).

9   On the view that what has been most influential in Descartes' method is not the simple (almost banal) rules, but rather the state or concentration of mind it has engendered for the analytic vivesection of nature and human nature,

Its method required the "purging" of all previously acquired and vague ideas; the courage to attempt to surmount the realm of the merely probable and versimilar; and, by implication, a political state unified enough to direct and plan (as in the Baconian version) this long-term rationalist project for the "possession and mastery of nature". In all these senses, then, neither Vico nor Oakeshott overstates the importance of Descartes' Rationalist challenge to schools and habits of practical wisdom.

But what about their critiques of Descartes' method? Both Vico and Oakeshott, recall, criticize Descartes' method—the rigorous analytic reduction to its basic elements of any problem and their expression in reduction specifiable in mathematical or mathematical-like symbols—as being incapable of accounting for its own activity. And Vico also, recall, criticizes the Cartesian purge and its pedagogic monopoly for a long-term reduction of the human mind, especially its imaginative, poetic, and inventive capacities, expertise which he says is stunted in the Cartesian substitution of algebraic for figurative geometry, and in the teaching of reductive analysis prior to the cultivation of the imaginative faculties, a development leading likely, says Vico, to widespread metaphysical and political skepticism.

Take first Vico's charge about the effects of teaching non-figurative, algebraic geometry to the young, i.e. that it leads to the loss of imagination, understood not merely as the capacity for pictorial representation, but more broadly as the capacity for invention and random association based on memory which results in creative problem-solving and in the creation of techniques such as Descartes' own. This issue (without reference to Vico) was addressed by Boyce Gibson in his 1932 book-length study of Descartes' philosophy. Drawing on some of Descartes' correspondence, Gibson addresses some "perplexing" quotations from Descartes' letters which suggest that at least in geometry (*though not physics*) Descartes thought that figurative representations could add to algebra as a means to further mathematical understanding:

> "To consider mathematical proportions better in particulars", he adds, "I thought I ought to put them in the form of lines, because... I could find no means of representing them more distinctly to my imagination and senses". *He further declares... that "extension, figures and movements can indeed be known by the understanding alone, but much better by the understanding aided by the imagination".* (Gibson, 1967, p. 189)

---

see Nietzsche's speculations (1967) on the psychological connections between modern experimental science and "ascetic ideals", especially Christian ones.

Gibson goes on to note that this sounds perplexing coming from Descartes, since he has taught us that imagination and memory of sense experience stand in the way of true knowledge in both science and metaphysics, requiring a "purgation of the scientific soul of its sensuous delusion". Yet he notes that while Descartes considered such a purge necessary for the study of metaphysics and physics (a field so often clouded by sense perception), geometry was a different case, since (unlike in everyday life) the senses *here* have no originative power and are less likely to cause error: "In geometry the initiative lies with the understanding, which projects its own conceptions into a sensuous form" (*ibid.*, p. 190).

Now, in defence of Vico on this point (who had not read Descartes' correspondence with Princess Elizabeth and Mersene), we might observe that Descartes *did* devise an algebraic analytic geometry as an alternative to synthetic figurative geometry; that he intended this analytic geometry to be instrumental in study of physics grounded in a purely intelligible realm; that, in general, he grounded possession of true knowledge in a purge of sense experience and its memory; and, finally, that it was Descartes' algebraic geometry which became the pedagogical inheritance of Cartesianism, and which Vico encountered in the curricula of his time. My general observation, in assessing the justice in Vico's claim, is that while it may not be exactly accurate in the letter, it is a fair criticism in spirit, since Descartes—in his contest with the dominant Scholaticism and neo-Aristotelianism of his day—never appears to have considered the fact that purging curricula of the humanistic literature and traditional geometry that he himself received from his Jesuit teachers would make it less likely that more characters with his abilities and insight might evolve on the human scene. Or, if Descartes did consider this prospect, he subjugated it to the overriding consideration of defeating the ubiquitous and entrenched "superstition" he saw being perpetuated by the scholastic philosophy and pedagogy, and the skepticism he saw engendered by humanistic thinkers like Montaigne and Charron.[10] Apparently, if the pedagogic and cultural outcome of the new method and philosophy was the appearance of characters with much narrowed sensibilities, then that was the price to be paid for the progress of the species.

There is another of Vico's criticisms of Cartesianism which still has force, even if excessively stated. This is his recognition that the new

---

[10] Gibson suggests that such rhetorical and political considerations were at least part of the reason that Descartes refused to countenance the idea of gradations of creation or intermediate unions of instinct and reason, of the animal and the spiritual (1967, pp. 186–214).

scientific mentality philosophically codified by Descartes intended to live no longer in the realm of probable and "verisimilar", but, insofar as possible, in the realm of the clear and certain as ascertained by a mathematical (and experimental) method, in the interest of the "mastery and possession of nature". Vico's defences of Aristotelian practical wisdom and rhetoric all hinge on the insight that the precision of science is not appropriate in the realm of politics and ethics (*praxis*), an orientation which, in spite of a few disclaimers to the contrary,[11] Descartes opposed himself, and sought as well to have opposed by those nurtured on the intellectual habits of his new method.

Let us look now at Oakeshott's general criticism of Descartes' method and the intellectual political habits it nourished over three centuries. Oakeshott's central criticism of Cartesianism, a utilitarian one we saw, is that it cannot give a complete account of its own activity, or of any concrete knowledge or skill, and hence is unskilful. (The Rationalist is like a man, says Oakeshott, "who first turns off the light and then complains because he cannot see" (1962, p. 32).) It cannot give such an account because, contrary to its teaching, there are no distinct beginning or ending points in experience; because it is not possible "to purge the mind" — there is no natural light of reason separable from what has previously been reasoned about; and because all knowledge cannot be formulated in rules and techniques, especially habits of timing, inventiveness, and judgment. The "rules" of any activity arise simultaneously with its practice, and should be separated from it and codified only in crises, and only as a critic, "never as the originator of action" (*ibid.*, p. 73). Furthermore, codes or methods are always abstracted from some concrete skill, and are destructive of other skills when applied to them in some abstract and universal way. In brief, practitioners of rationalist codes destroy or reduce concrete activities in the overriding interest of certainty and control over nature, events, and other human beings.

It is interesting to speculate about Descartes' responses to this litany of charges. On the issue of the purge of the mind by "natural light of reason", it is clear that Descartes would not budge. It is the basis for the surety of the "cogito" and the surety of God's existence, and the key to the reality behind the world apprehended by the senses, for him. But on issue of the "method" Descartes was less rigid than those who came after him and were nurtured exclusively on it. He clearly goes outside the method in his *Meditations*, returning on occasion to syllogistic

---

[11] For some examples, see Gibson (1967, pp. 345–349).

reasoning;[12] we have seen him reintroduce figurative and imaginative thinking as complements to the algebraic geometry he codified; and he was wont to caution prudence in moral and political matters, at least until certain knowledge was established.[13] Still it is difficult to see how Descartes could ever accept Oakeshott's arguments about practical knowledge (knowledge not susceptible to formulation in rules and techniques), and the loss of practical skill entailed in Rationalist approaches to learning, without giving up the central arguments of *The Discourse on the Method* and *The Regulae*. Perhaps Descartes might object that the introduction of a unified method into the realm of ethics and politics before the achievement of a detailed knowledge of human nature was never his intention. But, then, it was also never his intention that atheists in the next century would build upon Descartes' own radical separation of the animal and spiritual in human beings, further to "animalize" the human (especially since he thought he had provided irrefutable proof for the existence of God). Rather, it would seem that for Descartes the excessive rhetorical emphasis on his method at the expense of practical wisdom was the political and moral price to pay for the overturning of neo-Aristotelian Scholasticism in the realms of theology, metaphysics, and physics.

References

Beck, L.J. (1952) *The Method of Descartes*, pp. 289–298, Oxford: Clarendon Press.

Foster, M.B. (1934) "The Christian Doctrine of Creation and the Rise of Modern National Science", *Mind*, Vol. 43, No. 173, pp. 446–468.

Gibson, A.B. (1967) *The Philosophy of Descartes*, pp. 181–214, 345–349, New York: Russell and Russell.

Habermas, J. (1968) *Knowledge and Human Interests*, Boston, MA: Beacon Press.

Lilla, M. (1993) *G.B. Vico: The Making of an Anti-Modern*, pp. 49, 158, 211–212, Cambridge, MA: Harvard University Press.

Menn, S. (1993) *Descartes and Augustine*, pp. 15–33, Cambridge: Cambridge University Press.

Nietzsche, F. (1967) *On the Genealogy of Morals*, Kaufmann, W. (trans.), New York: Vintage Books.

Oakeshott, M.J. (1962) *Rationalism in Politics and Other Essays*, London: Methuen and Co.

---

[12] For a brief and guarded attempt to view the *Mediations* as no exception to Descartes' rules of method, see Beck (1952, pp. 289–298).

[13] See Gibson (1967, pp. 345–346).

Smith, N.K. (1952) *Descartes' Philosophical Writings*, London: MacMillan and Co.

Verene, D. (1981) *Vico's Science of Imagination*, p. 30, Ithaca, NY: Cornell University Press.

Vico, G.B. (1990) *On the Study Methods of Our Time*, pp. 13–14, Gianturco, E. (trans.), Ithaca, NY: Cornell University Press.

Five

Oakeshott, Strauss, and the Romans

"The expression 'the ancient world' which puts Greeks and Romans together, is one of the most misleading generalizations ever made." — Michael Oakeshott.

"But the Romans distinguished themselves above all other peoples by the regard... paid to the individual... and to the inviolable rights of all members of the state." —J. J. Rousseau.

The subject of this essay is a puzzle—why did Strauss and his contemporary students (in contrast to Oakeshott) give such short shrift to the Romans in their reconstruction of the history of Western higher reflection on politics and governance? Is it because, except possibly for Cicero, Roman thought does not rise to the level of philosophic thought? Or is it for other, and more prudential, reasons? And, as a corollary, why their *silence* (except for Strauss's very brief book review) on Charles McIlwain's well-known thesis (1940) that modern constitutional thought begins with Cicero's reflections on actual Roman practice, followed by the Straussian practice of lumping Cicero into the "classical" or "ancient" view, in order then to leap directly into "modern" political thought without any discussion of Roman influence on the modern view, especially that of Locke? And, finally and by contrast, why did Oakeshott (following McIlwain and others) place such emphasis on Roman and medieval legal thought and practice in his reconstruction of Western political theory, a subject on which Strauss is (not so much critical as) largely silent?

In what follows, I shall explore these questions by stages. First a summary of McIlwain's argument in *Constitutionalism: Ancient and Modern*; then a summary and exploration of Strauss's brief review of McIlwain's book; then a summary exploration of Oakeshott's LSE lectures on Roman (and medieval) political and legal thought; and finally some explicit conjecture, in the light of this material, on why

Strauss might have been silent on the Romans, and also what is lost for students in teaching the history of Western political theory without the Romans.

I. McIlwain on Greeks and the Romans

In 1940, Harvard Professor Charles Howard McIlwain caused to be published a series of six lectures he had just given under the title *Constitutionalism: Ancient and Modern,*[1] an urgent subject at the time given the attacks upon constitutionalism by both the extreme European right and left. McIlwain was also concerned to contest the views of Otto von Gierke about the Germanic origins of popular governance, by reminding readers of the influence of ancient Roman republicanism on modern British and European governmental and judicial practice. For our purposes here, I shall concentrate on McIlwain's second lecture, "The Ancient Conception of a Constitution", where he is careful to distinguish the Greek from the Roman inheritance, and follows Thomas Carlyle in suggesting that, "the dividing line between the ancient and modern political theory must be sought, if anywhere, in the period between Aristotle and Cicero" (McIlwain, 2007, p. 40).

McIlwain's central point about the differences between Greek and Roman ideas on meaning of a constitution (*politeia, constitutio*) is that for the Greeks it referred to a comprehensive way of life in its totality:

> It is a term which compromises all the innumerable characteristics which determine that state's peculiar nature... its whole economic and social texture as well as matters governmental in our narrower modern sense. (*ibid.*, p. 26)

He also notes that the Greeks saw a close analogy between the polity and the organism of a human being, and that every constitution had its accompanying *ethos* which moulded citizen virtue to its contours. He quotes Isocrates that the *politeia* is the "*psyche* of the *polis*" with "power over it like that of the mind over the body". He cites Aristotle that the *politeia* is "in a sense the life of the city" (*ibid.*, p. 27). Aristotle also observes[2] that the laws are made to suit the constitution and not the other way around (Aristotle, 1984, p. 119).

---

[1] McIlwain had already written a previous work, *The Growth of Political Thought in the West* (New York: Macmillan, 1932), with a lucid chapter on the Romans, which contains the following characterization: "...in Roman hands doctrines drawn from rival schools tended to be thrown together to make a working political creed rather than a system coherent in all its parts" (p. 105).

[2] For more on this from an historical perspective, see Hansen (1991, pp. 64–65). McIlwain does not discuss Aristotle on this point.

When he comes to the Romans, McIlwain is concerned to show, *contra* fashionable *fin de siècle* scholarship, that the real Roman bequeathal to European governance was not the autocratic practices of the later empire, but the constitutional theory and practice of the republic in its prime. His major point is that the Romans had a different conception of a constitution from the Greek *politeia* for two main reasons. *First*, the Romans saw the source of all authority in the definition of law (*lex*), as an enactment of the *whole* Roman people: "SPQR means senate and *populus*, not the senate and any assembly even roughly representing the people" (McIlwain, 2007, p. 43). (Contrast the legal abstraction of this thought with Aristotle for whom whoever rules is the regime.) And second, the Romans made a distinction between public and private law (*jus publicum* and *jus privatum*), both of them referring to the "natural person" but under different aspects. McIlwain quotes the nineteenth-century German scholar, von Ihering, to the effect that "the sole difference between them lies in the fact that private rights affect private individuals exclusively, while all the individuals alike participate in the public". Again, following von Ihering, McIlwain notes that the general principles were the same in both public and private law — "the primary notion of each is the independence of the individual", and it was "only after a long and bitter struggle that the dominance of the state" over the individual was finally established (*ibid.*, p. 44).[3]

---

3   Rudolph von Ihering's *Geist des Römischen Recht* (1872) has never been translated into English or even transposed from old German script, but there are some English summaries of its main themes. See, for example, Radin (1924, p. 393) who says that von Ihering thought that the Roman law had as "its keynote" the idea of a purely "mechanical" equality, "owing to the tyranny of an abstract rule", and that the spirit of Roman law could be regarded "as a rigid selfishness which, however, sacrificed the lower and individual advantage to that of the organization in which he could reach his largest development". Arguably this *ethos* of selfishness elevated by legal coercion is what Machiavelli is praising in the *Discourses* on Livy, a subject which Strauss never addresses, as we shall see. McIllwain is silent on this whole subject and clearly did not want to discuss von Iherings's claim about the "selfishness" of Roman law in praising Roman constitutionalism, except to note that the idea of rights grows out of property disputes. Von Ihering's own argument in the three volume work is that (1) for the Romans the source of law was not the state but the subjective will of the individual personality, hence the importance of property (and property law) and self-reliance as expressions of the individual creative will; and (2) that this individual egoism (*egoismus*) was mitigated by the family (the source of Roman morality) and by a civic *ethos* in the republican era for the "free surrender" of the individual to the state. Deutsche-archiv, online, 3 vols. Vol II, pp. 118, 129, 130, 157, 208, 239. See also note #4 below.

A corollary of McIlwain's emphasis on private rights under Roman law is that the "spirit" of Roman republican law becomes apparent in legal disputes over property (McIlwain, 2007, p. 56).[4] This claim will become important in our subsequent analysis of Cicero's assertion that the state exists to protect private property.

II. Strauss on McIlwain and the Romans

Let us turn now to Strauss's brief review of McIlwain's book, included along with many others of his 1940s reviews in *What is Political Philosophy?* (1959). Strauss devotes the first two of a three-paragraph review to summarizing and contextualizing McIlwain's argument, noting its criticisms of Montesquieu's imaginative, functional separation of powers as the basis of English liberty, and McIlwain's preference for the English medieval practice of an energetic executive limited by an independent judiciary preserving individual rights (*gubernaculum* and *jurisdictio*). Strauss also notes here (justly!) that McIlwain's attempt to divide ancient from modern constitutionalism on the basis of "organic growth" *vs.* rational "blueprint" cannot satisfactorily account for Aristotle's views in *The Politics*.

In the last paragraph, however, Strauss addresses partially and cryptically our concern in this exploration. He notes that McIlwain "evidently prefers" the opinion (Carlyle's) that the "dividing line between the ancient and modern conception of constitutionalism" should be sought "in the period between Aristotle and Cicero", and is of Roman and Stoic origin (Strauss, 1959, p. 271). Strauss then says that "this judgment does not seem to be warranted", and that "one may wonder" whether this dividing line shouldn't be sought in a novel doctrine of the later sixteenth and seventeenth centuries, consciously opposed to ancient and medieval doctrines. He also suggests cryptically that McIlwain's description of the difference "between medieval and modern constitutionalism is apt to confirm... that suspicion"[5] (*ibid.*, p. 272). For our purposes it is important to note that

---

4   In drawing out the influence on medieval Europe of Roman legal ideas on property, McIlwain observes that even the issue of the king's prerogative was treated in judicial discussions under the general rules of the proprietary rights of any subject of the realm.

5   It is difficult to know what to make of Strauss's abbreviated suggestion that McIlwain's description of the differences between medieval and modern constitutionalism ought to lead one to suspect that "modernity" begins in novel doctrines of the late sixteenth and seventeenth centuries (a favourite Straussian theme). McIlwain's discussion of the transition to modern constitutionalism is limited to the struggle in Britain between *gubernaculum* and *jurisdictio* to "swallow" one another, especially the former, as Tudor and

Strauss never addresses McIlwain's fundamental claim (and, later, Oakeshott's) about the differences between Greek and Roman constitutionalism — rather he simply deflects that question by moving on to the question of when "modernity" began. And if Strauss's "modernity" is to be defined as the dethronement of the contemplative life in political philosophy, then (as we shall see) to be persuasive it must confront the Ciceronian and Roman criticism of the claim for superiority of the contemplative life as depicted in *De Officiis*.

It might be expected that there would be some analysis of Roman political thought and practice in Strauss's work on Machiavelli's use of Livy's discourses on the Roman republic, but this turns out not to be the case. Rather, in his writing on Machiavelli, Strauss is concerned to view him as the "founder" of modernity in "dethroning" the contemplative life as the *telos* of political reflection. Most of Strauss's account is an attempt to cast Machiavelli as a Latin Averroist (like Marsilius of Padua before him and Locke after him) who saw the incompatibility of philosophy and revealed religion, and who was prepared to overturn the "classical" and biblical tradition in order to displace Christianity with a more salutary and patriotic civil religion which might help liberate the Italian city-states from northern European and Papal domination. (In the words of Strauss scholar Catherine Zuckert, "Strauss used Machiavelli in the way he thought Machiavelli had used Livy, to advance his own argument" (Zuckert, 2013, p. 4).[6] Yet as we shall see below, Strauss is silent on the features of Roman and Ciceronian thought which make a similar critique of Platonic and Aristotelian views on the function and utility of philosophic reflection.

Stuart monarchs attempted to strengthen their control cover their realms. McIlwain says they were largely unsuccessful in this attempt owing to (1) the deep-seated practice of (and belief in) British proprietary rights (echoing Rome), and (2) the disunity introduced into the people at large by the Protestant Reformation. He does note two novel features in these developments — (1) the growing acceptance that Parliament could speak for the entire people, and (2) the idea that a law might be illegitimate (not merely unjust) if it contradicted natural law.

6   For a similar view with regard to Oakeshott (on the Romans), see Callahan (2012, p. 186) who asks why, "in painting his flattering portrait of Roman political experience", Oakeshott chose to gloss over the "darker episodes in Roman history". Callahan's conjecture is that Oakeshott saw these of trivial significance in his account of "what was singular and admirable" in the Roman political experience.

III. Oakeshott on the Romans

Oakeshott's account of Roman political experience in his year-long course on the history of political thought at LSE in the 1960s and 1970s has similarities with McIlwain's account of the good influences on Europe of Roman republican constitutionalism and with many of the nineteenth-century German and English scholars whom McIlwain relies on, although Oakeshott's account is more generally and insight-fully written (Oakshott placed McIlwain's book on constitutionalism, as well as his earlier book on the development of Western political thought, on the syllabus for the course) (O'Sullivan, 2003, p. 186). Rather than try to summarize all of Oakeshott's lectures on the Romans, let us focus for our purposes on his accounts of the differences between the Greek and Roman outlook on the state and constitutional law.

Oakeshott begins with the hyperbolic assertions that (1) the Romans were arguably "the only European people to show a genuine genius for government and politics", and (2) that, in most respects, "the political experience of the Romans was utterly unlike that of ancient Greece". Furthermore, he says that the expression "'the ancient world'", con-flating Greeks and Romans, "is one of the most misleading generaliza-tions ever made" (Oakeshott, 2006, p. 176).

Now, what were the major differences between the Greek and Roman political experiences to which Oakeshott is alluding here? Besides the obvious fact that Greek politics was the politics of a "world" of independent and diverse city-states, and Roman politics that of a single city-state enduring for a millennium, there are several differences relevant to our exploration here.

For one thing, Oakeshott observes that while Greeks (especially Aristotle) had rejected the idea of the *family* as the analogy for political reflection, the Romans employed it, seeing governance as an extension of family discipline. The Romans thought of themselves as a single, extended family (the *populus Romanus*) created initially as a partnership among tribes by a treaty (*foedus*) or contract,[7] as well as a sacred part-nership (*communio sacrorum*) with the (family) gods to obtain their support through performance of sacred rites. This "poetic" account of their origins also leads Oakeshott to observe that while the political self-consciousness of the Greeks was achieved by philosophers with

---

[7] Aristotle explicitly rejected, by contrast, the (Sophist) idea of a social compact as the analogy for the basis of the *polis*, arguing that it reduced its political friendship to the loose partnership of a military or commercial alliance. See Aristotle (1984, p. 99).

little interest in historic origins,[8] Roman political self-consciousness was achieved by "historians, poets, and lawyers, not philosophers". This fact was also conducive to the Roman generation of a legend or myth about the destiny of the Roman people to civilize the world, a legend[9] which gave the Roman people a degree of unity (for a millennium) lacking in the Greek experience. (What broke this family destiny and unity, for Oakeshott, was the extension of citizenship to unmanageable limits under the later empire, and the tension introduced between religion and politics by the adoption of Christianity as the official state religion — Oakeshott, 2006, pp. 208–221).

Another important difference between Romans and Greeks for Oakeshott (following McIlwain here) was a clear and concise distinction between the public and private aspects of community, lacking in the vague Greek spatial distinction between *agora* and household. The Romans, says Oakeshott, recognized a distinction between "public law" and "private law" (including an elaborate body of private property law), "which the Athenians never quite managed to make" (*ibid.*, p. 223). They were united by the *general* idea to keep faith with one another to preserve the traditions (*mos maiorum*) of the ancestors, and this is why for Oakeshott they constituted a "civil association" rather than a more purposive Greek political association. In an insightful paragraph (which prefigures Oakeshott's later distinction between *societas* and *universitas*), Oakeshott lays out what he means by "civil association":

> The Romans had what the Athenians never had, namely the notion that they composed a civil association. What united them was not engagement in a common enterprise, but respect for... ancient customs, and... for the *law*. And this law was not thought of as the organization of an enterprise, but as the terms in which they kept faith with one another. (Oakeshott, 2006, p. 212)

In my view, Oakeshott is implying here (and elsewhere) that although the Greeks, and especially the Athenians, were more philosophic in their intellectual orientation, the Romans were actually more capable of abstraction and formalism, especially with regard to legal matters, a rare quality in any civilization. Unlike the Athenians and Strauss, the

---

[8]   *Apropos* of this claim, consider Aristotle's dramatically brief "history" of the development of the *polis* — that it comes into existence from necessity, but *exists* for the good life (*Politics*, 1984, p. 37).

[9]   *Apropos* of the importance of legend and myth in maintaining the unity of the political community, Oakeshott notes: "The philosophical talents of the Romans may have been small... but they... did not lack the power to understand their political experience in the idiom of general ideas" (Oakeshott, 2006, p. 207).

Romans (and later Hobbes) were impressed with the *procedural* basis for the *legitimacy* of sovereign authority, which derived from following established and agreed-upon procedures. What Oakeshott calls the "rule of law" (nomocracy) in modern European political experience is meant to recall the Roman view of law as *general* considerations and conditions to be observed in both private and public pursuits, *versus* the Greek (and Aristotelian) view that laws are made to further the *ethos* and particular purposes of the ruling regime and its conception of justice (teleocracy). And this generalization extends as well to the administration of law. The Athenians, in particular, "did not distinguish between politics and administration" (Hansen, 1991, p. 76). Oakeshott's concern about "modernity" is not the Straussian one over its moral relativism, but rather that by returning to the Greek view of politics as the pursuit of the "good life" it would lose the Roman insight into the difference between *authority* of law and mere *power* to achieve political projects, an insight (in combination with a sense of irony to deflate ideological enthusiasm) necessary for the preservation of liberal freedoms.

IV. Cicero on the Romans

I have attempted thus far to present enough of the views of McIlwain and Oakeshott to show the problems with Strauss's lumping Roman political thought in with Greek political philosophic speculation under the rubric of the "ancient" or "classical" views. I would now like to show that many of the views Strauss labels as "modern" in their utilitarian rejection of the superiority of the contemplative life can be found in the contemporary Ciceronian writing, in particular his work on duties, *De Officiis*, written in his own name as a letter to his son who was studying philosophy at the time in Athens (while Cicero was on the run from Mark Anthony's assassins after the death of Caesar and the fall of the republic). The theme of the work is a common, contemporary rhetorical one, that there is only *apparent* contradiction between what is expedient (*utile*) and what is morally right (*honestum*), but in making this case Cicero has occasion to articulate typical Roman views of the problems with Greek and Platonic political philosophy as well as on the purpose of the state.

My general aim in exploring these themes is to suggest that they are all ones which Strauss and his students have attributed *de novo* to modern writers such as Machiavelli and Locke.[10] These three themes

---

10　For a sustained "Straussian" account of the leap from ancient to modern which is silent on Cicero's criticisms of Greek philosophy, see Pangle (1988), who makes no mention of, nor engages with, Cicero's criticisms of Plato, his

are (1) the superiority of the political to the philosophic life; (2) the role of the will or "willing" in morality and hence the importance of wilfully "keeping faith" with the parties to one's contracts; and (3) the protection of private property as the just purpose of the state. Cicero, a Roman lawyer and orator educated by Greeks in its various schools of philosophy, drew eclectically upon whichever philosophic teachings would improve his abilities as a political and forensic orator, though his preferences were the schools of Plato, Aristotle, and the Stoics, with an *animus* against the Epicureans and the Cynics. In *De Officiis* he argues explicitly for the centrality of moral duties in philosophic speculation, and says that to be drawn away from the "active life" is contrary to moral duty, refusing to identify the contemplative life as the most active life, in the fashion of Aristotle. He calls philosophers "traitors to social life", saying they fall into injustice in declining to care for the welfare of their fellow men, and specifically criticizing Plato's philosophers (in the *Republic*) for being forced to return to the cave and care for others; "for hampered by their pursuit of learning they leave to their fate those whom they ought to defend" (Cicero, 1975, p. 29).[11]

Cicero's defence of the "active life", and the superiority of political and military leaders to contemplative philosophers, is telling in the way he reasons. Unlike Aristotle, for example, who reasons in the *Nicomachean Ethics* that the contemplative life is superior to the political life because it is more divine-like and more self-sufficient in imitating the Unmoved Mover who thinks only thought, Cicero reasons in a practical, Roman utilitarian fashion that orators and generals are greater because their actions affect the lives of more people and for longer periods of time. This is also the basis for preferring the statesman and lawyers over the military commanders: "For Themistocles' victory (at Salamis) served the state only once, while Solon's work will be of service forever... for the war was directed by the courses of that Senate which Solon had created." And, more generally, the function of

---

defence of the active over the contemplative life, his utilitarian view of the "uses" of philosophy, and his defence of private property. Pangle is generally inclined to highlight the utilitarian and bourgeois features of Machiavelli and Locke as something novel rather than Roman, in order to suggest a conflict between the acquisition of wealth and civic duty, a conflict which the Romans and Cicero (and George Washington!) did not think existed. For the "strains" in Strauss's attempt to portray Marsilius, Machiavelli, and Locke as Latin Averroists, see Zuckert and Zuckert (2014, pp. 191–214).

11   In *The Republic* of Plato, Socrates says that to existing cities philosophers are not obligated since they were educated against the will of the city (1968, p. 198).

virtue for the Roman Cicero is never for its own sake, but "to win the hearts of men and attach men to our service" (Cicero, 1975, p. 33).

Cicero also reasons of Plato's philosophers that it would be better if they performed civic duties of their own accord, "for an action intrinsically right is just only on condition that it is voluntary" or of their own will (*voluntas*). Cicero does not say more about this in *De Officiis* but in *De Fato* he waxes on about the independence of the will or voluntary motions (*motus voluntarios*) of the mind, which are self-caused:

> ...voluntary motion possesses the intrinsic property of being in our power and of obeying us, and its obedience is not uncaused, for its nature itself the cause of this. (Cicero, 2001, p. 221)

Now, this Ciceronian discussion of role of will (*voluntas*) in morality is important for our purposes because it does not occur in Greek ethical thought (not even in Aristotle's intellectualist account of choice, *proairesis*, as an appetite guided by deliberation and especially not in the view of the Platonic Socrates for whom wrong choice is always a matter of ignorance). The Roman emphasis on will (backed up by a sworn oath) is the basis for the power of the practice of "keeping faith" with other partners in the community to observe the old ways (*mos maiorum*) of the ancestors. It was arguably the "glue" which provided the unity of the *populus Romanus* for centuries.

Another distinctively Ciceronian and Roman idea set forth in *De Officiis* which occurs in modern, especially Lockean, writing is the assertion that the state exists to protect private property (one's own), and to maintain the difference between the public and the private (*res publica* and *res privata*), the conflation of which by Caesar was a source of Cicero's *animus* against him.

Here are some of Cicero's assertions on this score:

> For the chief purpose of the establishment on the constitutional state and government (*res publicae civitatesque constitutae*) was that individual property rights might be secured... it was in the hope of safeguarding their possessions that they sought the protection of cities.
>
> The man in administrative office us must make it his first care... that private citizens suffer no invasion of their property rights by acts of the state. (Cicero, 1975, p. 249)

Apropos of theses Ciceronian arguments is Sir Henry Maine's apt observations in 1861 on Locke's *Second Treatise*:

> The Lockeian theory of the origin of Law in a Social Compact scarcely conceals its Roman derivation, and indeed is only the dress by which ancient views were rendered more attractive to a particular generation of the moderns... (Maine, 1861, p. 144)

Hopefully, the material summarized thus far from McIlwain, Oakeshott, and Cicero has been sufficient to establish that the Straussian silence concerning the Roman influences on modernity is, at the least, puzzling. Let us turn now to conjecture on the reasons for this silence.

V. Conclusion: Conjustures on the Reasons for the Straussian Silence concerning the Romans

The "novel" doctrine of modernity for Strauss was arguably not the dethronement of the contemplative life and the ascension of the practical life itself, for the Romans (and medievalists such as Duns Scotus) had already done this, and Strauss knew it. The "novel" feature of modernity for Strauss was arguably the secular defence of the Christian separation of politics and morality.[12] In the interest of his country, Machiavelli was forced to teach princes "how not to be good" because the gap between morality and the requisite minimum for public order had been so widened by the Christian teaching of the gospels ("resist not evil") that what was a plausible stretch for Cicero between moral rectitude and expediency was no longer a plausible option for Machiavelli.

That is, Cicero could make such a plausible case that the morally good (*honestum*) and expedient (*utile*) do not ultimately diverge because his (and the Roman) understanding of moral goodness was already infused with what was good for the state. This is why, for Cicero, it is *honestum* to kill a tyrant and take his possessions for the state, because the ancient Roman understanding of morality was inseparable from what was good for the Roman political order in the way that the Christian, perfectionist, *apolitical* morality was not, in spite of attempts by neo-Romans such as Aquinas to narrow the gap.[13] Arguably, for

---

12   In my view, Strauss's indictment of "creativity" as the root of modern darkness is also an indictment of the effects of Christian teaching and symbolism, both popularizing and expanding the Jewish biblical account of the Creation. If "creativity" is understood, following Strauss, as an extension of theoretical knowledge into the realms of *praxis* and production, then arguably the Christian symbolism of the Incarnation (the *logos* become material) has facilitated this development, as well as the demand for actualization of theory in practice and production. The problem for Strauss here is that it has also facilitated the advance of modern scientific (including medical) knowledge and practice, an at least ambiguously beneficial development for humanity. See, on this, Foster (1934).

13   Thus, Strauss would appear on this point to agree with Rousseau that since Jesus appeared no good politics or polity has been possible, though Strauss was certainly prepared to defend liberal democracy (as a better of worse outcomes) for its incorporation of salutary pre-modern themes. The

Strauss to have separated out the Romans from the "ancient" or "classical" view would have diminished the force of his implied indictment that the root of "modern darkness" be traced to the teaching of Jesus "to be perfect as your father in heaven", which had the effect over centuries of making realistic morality impossible by aiming too high for most people (a criticism he thought not extendable to Judaism and Islam as religions of law).

Yet a plausible argument[14] might be made (1) that the ills of modernity could *also* be traced (following the Platonic teaching) to modernity's subversion of morality by the cumulative, long-term, commercial, democratic liberation and expansion of the appetites (Coats, 2016), and (2) that (especially Protestant) Christianity's separation of morality and politics has *merely* facilitated this development in the interest of removing barriers to the accumulation of scientific and technological knowledge.[15]

Straussian teaching on Machiavelli also included the argument fleshed out by the French Straussian, Pierre Manent (1994, pp. 10–11), that in order to diminish the power of the Roman Catholic Church, Machiavelli had to discredit Aristotelianism as well as biblical authority, since Aquinas had completed Aristotle's teleological hierarchy of natural virtues with the supernatural virtues, which were under the care of the Church hierarchy. In order to do this, Machiavelli reduced political science to efficient causality solely, for the sake of certainty and control over extreme cases, in the fashion of (but also in advance of) modern science. On this novel feature of Machiavelli's thought, I am in agreement with the Straussians. See Coats (2003).

[14] Yet another of the causes of "modern darkness" (a term Strauss used in correspondence with Eric Vogelin) could have been the misguided fascist attempt to return to Roman and Germanic martial virtue as a remedy for the moral decline of a technologically and commercially advanced, liberal democratic civilization. However, addressing this would only have muddied the explanatory waters for Strauss, since he is implying that Machiavelli's political science and fascism both were occasioned by the long-term effects of the Christian (and later liberal) separation of morality and politics, a phenomenon exacerbated by nineteenth-century historicist theory of the temporality of all knowledge ("Modern philosophy is... the secularized form of Christianity" —Strauss, 1959, p. 128). For a more nuanced, but related, perspective on the rise of "modernity" see the French-Swiss medieval scholar Andre de Muralt, who argues that "modernity" began in the thirteenth century with the medieval voluntarists, Scotus and (also nominalist) Ockham, and their implicit equation *of* human willing (without a *telos*) *and* God's unbounded creative will (also without a *telos*) (de Muralt, 1991, p. 39). See also Lobkowicz (1967, pp. 77–78) on Scotus's view of the extension of theoretical knowledge into the practical realm.

[15] The Zuckerts (2014, pp. 163–164) argue that, by implication, Strauss saw "modernity" as arising from a combination of biblical and Aristotelian

If this analysis is even only partially correct about the origins of the ills of "modernity", then an appreciation of the Roman jurisprudential insights into the importance of the procedural rule of law in checking democracy's excesses is all the more necessary, and all the more reason in teaching the history of higher Western political reflection to include in it the study of Roman constitutional thought, as did Oakeshott and McIllwain and most of the Anglo-American legal tradition. For, arguably, the perfectionist tendencies of Greek philosophy extended into Greek forensic and legal reasoning with deleterious effect, as Sir Henry Maine observed a century and a half ago based on this reading of examples in Aristotle's *Rhetoric*:

> The Greek intellect, with all its nobility and elasticity, was quite unable to confine itself within the strait waistcoat of a legal formula... questions of pure law were constantly argued on every consideration which could possibly influence the mind of the judges. *No durable system of jurisprudence could be produced... this way.*
>
> A community which never hesitated to relax rules of written law whenever they stood in the way of an ideally perfect decision on the facts of a particular case... would contain no framework to which... conceptions of future ages could be fitted. (Maine, 1861, pp. 75–76)

References

Aristotle (1984) *The Politics*, Lord, C. (trans.), Chicago, IL: University of Chicago Press.

Callahan, G. (2012) *Oakeshott on Rome and America*, Exeter: Imprint Academic.

Cicero (1975) *De Officiis*, Cambridge, MA: Harvard University Press.

Cicero (2001) "De Fato", in *Cicero IV*, Cambridge, MA: Harvard University Press.

---

teachings, owing to Aristotle's view that moral virtue could be for its own sake. But this cannot be correct about Aristotle. (Moreover, it is the Platonic Socrates who speaks in *The Republic* of justice belonging to the class of the best things—those done both for their own sake and for their consequences.) Although Aristotle occasionally speaks of *praxis* for its own sake when contrasting it with production, his comprehensive view (*Metaphysics*, XII) is clearly that *only* the activity of thought acting upon thought can be *solely* for its own sake. (Yet for Strauss's exoteric, Judaicized Aristotle, "the political", not the "metaphysical", is the "first philosophy".) A more defensible view here is that of Foster (1934) that modern science (if not "modernity") arises from the late medieval *combination of* biblical, creationist cosmology's account of the reality and mystery of matter, *with* a Greek logic and mathematics which are no longer futilely employed to attempt a *logos* of matter, but rather to make predictions about its probable movements, thus displacing a teleological worldview.

Coats, W.J. (2003) "Machiavelli as Classical Roman Rhetorician?", in Coats, W.J., *Political Theory and Practice*, London: Associated University Presses.

Coats, W.J. (2003) "On the Actualization of the Best Regimes in Plato's Political Dialogues", in Coats, W.J., *Political Theory and Practice*, London: Associated University Press.

Coats, W.J. (2016) "Groundwork for a Theory of Republican Character in a Democratic Age", in Kellow, G. & Leddy, N. (eds.) *On Civic Republicanism*, Toronto: Toronto University Press.

Emberly, P. & Cooper, B. (eds.) (1993) *Faith and Political Philosophy: The Correspondence between Leo Strauss and Eric Voegelin, 1934–1964*, Columbia, MO: University of Missouri Press.

Foster, M.B. (1934) "The Christian Doctrine of Creation and the Rise of Modern Natural Science", *Mind*, Vol. 43 (Oct).

Hansen, M. (1991) *The Athenian Democracy in The Age of Demothenes*, Oxford: Blackwell.

Ihering, R. (1878) *Geist des Römischen Recht*, Leipzig: Brestkoph and Härtel.

Lobkowicz, N. (1967) *Theory and Practice: History of a Concept from Aristotle to Marx*, Indianapolis, IN: Notre Dame Press.

Manent, P. (1994) *Intellectual History of Liberalism*, Princeton, NJ: Princeton University Press.

McIlwain, C.H. (2007) *Constitutionalism: Ancient and Modern*, Indianapolis, IN: Liberty Fund.

McIlwain, C.H. (1932) *The Growth of Political Thought in the West*, New York: Macmillan.

Maine, H.S. (1861) *Ancient Law*, London: John Murray.

de Muralt, A. (1991) *L'Enjeu de la Philosophie Medievale*, Leiden: E.J. Brill.

Orren K. & Skowronek (2017) *The Policy State*, Cambridge, MA: Harvard University Press.

O'Sullivan, L. (2003) *Oakeshott on History*, Exeter: Imprint Academic.

Oakeshott, M.J. (2006) *Lectures on the History of Political Thought*, Exeter: Imprint Academic.

Pangle, T.L. (1988) *The Spirit of Modern Republicanism*, Chicago, IL: University of Chicago Press.

Plato (1968) *The Republic*, Bloom, A. (trans.), New York: Basic Books.

Rabin, M. (1974) "Fundamental Concepts of Roman Law", *California Law Review*, Vol. 12, 514.

Strauss, L. (1952) "On Collingwood's *Philosophy of History*", *Review of Metaphysics*, Vol. 5, 4, June.

Strauss, L. (1959) *What is Political Philosophy?*, Westport, CT: Greenwood Press.

Strauss, L. (1972) "Niccolo Machiavelli", in Strauss, L. & Cropsey, J., *History of Political Philosophy*, Chicago, IL: Rand McNally.

Zuckert, C.H. (2013) "Machiavelli's Democratic Republic", paper presented to *Conference on Study of Political Thought*, Yale University.

Zuckert, M.P. & Zuckert, C.H. (2014) *Leo Strauss and the Problem of Political Philosophy*, Chicago, IL: University of Chicago Press.

Six

Reply to Liddington
on Oakeshott

This essay is a reply to some extensive and sustained criticisms by John Liddington[1] of Oakeshott's account of both experience and of the modern state in *Experience and Its Modes* (1933) and *On Human Conduct* (1975), respectively. In the former case Liddington uses techniques of modern analytic philosophy to attempt to identify logical contradictions in Oakeshott's arguments, and defend instead a realist view of truth as conformity or correspondence of the mind to reality, in opposition to Oakeshott's Idealist coherence theory of truth. In the latter case, Liddington attempts to show logical contradictions in Oakeshott's account of the modern state as subsisting in the tension between civil and enterprise association, and promises an alternative account which he never fully gets round to. This essay also replies briefly to Liddington's critique of Oakeshott's criticisms of modern rationalism.

There are some general considerations contributing to the differences between Oakeshott and Liddington on these subjects which should be noted before proceeding. One is Oakeshott's (sometimes mischievous) use of the literary trope of hyperbole in presenting his philosophic case. In this mixing of philosophy and rhetoric, Oakeshott follows the example of writers such as (the later) Hobbes and Rousseau.[2] Yet Liddington always simply takes Oakeshott's rhetorical

---

[1] These are contained in a 1985 unpublished Oxford University doctoral thesis (begun in the 1970s) which Oakeshott was initially helpful with, and in a published article developing some of the themes of the thesis. See "References" for details.

[2] Examples of Oakeshottian hyperbole: (1) "that philosophy is without any direct bearing upon the practical conduct of life" (Oakeshott, 1933, p. 1), when *Experience and Its Modes* repeatedly conveys that while philosophy cannot tell us what to do, it can tell us what not to do, tell us when we are being irrelevant; (2) saying that civil association is *not* in pursuit of a common purpose and is indifferent to the outcomes of specific performances (Oakeshott, 1975, p. 182), when his comprehensive view is that there

exaggerations at face value and points out problems with them, declining to grant Oakeshott poetic licence. To take a Hobbesian illustration of this issue, when Hobbes says that "covenants without the sword are but words", we can see that this is clearly not so in many cases, but we may grant the exaggeration as an artful way of conveying that in extreme and foundational cases power and legitimacy may coincide. Liddington's characteristic method would be not to concede this point, but to begin pointing out the various instances in which covenants might be observed without the credible threat of force.

Another general consideration contributing to differences between Oakeshott and Liddington (and with many other critics as well) is Oakeshott's reluctance fully to define terms he is employing, preferring instead to illustrate their meaning in the way he employs them in exposition and argument. In particular, as we shall see, Oakeshott's use of the terms "formal" and "substantive" will become relevant here, as well as the undefined difference between *general* and *substantive* purposes. Yet another general consideration is Oakeshott's often playfully eccentric nomenclature such as his use of the term "moral" as synonymous with formal or general. And yet another is Oakeshott's penchant for leaping from one level of generality in his exposition to another, often creating the impression of self-contradiction, for example using "individual" in practical discourse to mean that which is isolated and self-contained, yet using "individual" in philosophic discourse to connote only the coherent whole of experience. A final difficulty (we shall see) is Oakeshott's penchant for contrasting two ideal types in analysis, rather than viewing them as points or degrees on a continuum, as, for example, the differences in degree between hot, tepid, cool, cold, etc. With these general considerations in mind, let us turn to Liddington's specific critiques.[3]

Liddington's chapters on *Experience and Its Modes* (1933) attempt to show that Oakeshott's Idealist account of experience is predicated on an argument he conceived to advance a particular conception of history (and the writing of history), which adopts a coherence (*vs.* correspondence) theory of truth and reality. Liddington concludes that a coherence applies only to deductive and analytic systems and is only partially applicable to the modality of history, and not at all to those of

---

is a difference between substantive purposes and general purposes or concerns such as security, peace, and moral virtue (*ibid.*, p. 119).

3   For example, formal vs. substantive, civil vs. enterprise association, *societas* vs. *universitas*, individual vs. individual manqué, explanatory vs. persuasive languages. An exception might be the politics of faith vs. the politics of skepticism, both of which are encouraged to move toward an Aristotelian mean.

science and practice, which theory forces Oakeshott into incoherence and contradiction in his arguments.

Liddington argues in this context that historical facts may be related to one another, but that these relations are not their entirety—that coherence among facts does not exhaust what they are (Liddington, 1985, pp. 47–52). In my view, Liddington does not *fully* see the constructivist or creativist nature of Oakeshott's account of both experience and its modalities. For Oakeshott, each method of knowing or experiencing creates (or is "correlative to") its own subject matter in the way each mediates experience (Oakeshott, 1983, p. 9).[4] This is the reason why established modes of experience (such as practice, history, science, and, later, art) cannot directly address one another—because they have no common subject matter to discuss. A physicist, for example, does not study a falling apple, *per se*—he/she first resolves the apple into an abstraction (with universal properties) called "mass" and then plugs its value into a formula such as "d=gt". The scientist must subsequently, in order to have a practical effect, find a way (more or less successfully) to reintegrate the deductive conclusions about "mass" into the world of falling apples. (Insofar as one can speculate on Oakeshott's motivations here they seem to be not so much an attempt to defend a particular conception of history, but to improve on Kant by insulating religious and historical claims from modern science without denying reason access to ultimate reality, through retention of the Hegelian-Idealist claim that the subject of judgments is a whole of which less than the whole is predicated.)

Yet Liddington continues to argue (replicating the classic debates between philosophic realism and idealism) that there is a world of things "out there" (similar to a Kantian *noumenal* realm, but more accessible) against which to hold ideas accountable in the degree to which they "correspond" to "reality". Otherwise, he says, positing truth as the coherence of mutually dependent parts cannot distinguish historical truth (or any truth) from a "coherent fantasy" (Liddington, 1985, p. 52). Yet, here again, Liddington does not seem to see that for

---

4   Although Oakeshott says that "every form of experience must create its own subject matter" (1933, p. 245), this is actually a loose, abbreviated way of speaking, for he sometimes says that the "character of what is experienced is correlative to the means in which it is experienced" (*ibid.*, p. 9), and that this is not a relationship of "cause and consequence". For Oakeshott, there is never an "it" in experience (*ibid.*, p. 31)—the form and content of experience, the manner of experiencing, and what is experienced are inseparable and arise simultaneously with neither more important than the other. In this sense, then, every form of experience creates its own subject matter.

Oakeshott the "coherence" criterion contains or comprehends the "correspondence" criterion (and not the other way around as Liddington and other realists would have it). For Oakeshott's "coherence" theory, if there is a conflict or contradiction between an historical narrative and the available evidence, then it is not coherent. What is historical fantasy and relatively coherent historical truth (always incomplete for Oakeshott) depends on the best evidence available to the historian at the present moment. (As Liddington correctly observes, there is no truth, *simpliciter* for Oakeshott — *ibid.*, p. 181.) As the available evidence changes with new discoveries, the application of the epithet "historical fantasy" in any particular case also changes.

As Oakeshott has it, there is never anything but a present world of ideas, but this world is never *merely* my world (as in solipsism). To be a "world" or a system of mutually dependent and reinforcing parts it must address the best (conventionally defined) available evidence and account for inconsistencies in any narrative which presents itself as true. In general, here and, as we shall see, in other instances as well, Oakeshott is often taking a more comprehensive or general viewpoint than his critics.

An illustration of Oakeshott's more "comprehensive" viewpoint may be found in Oakeshott's 1949 review of J.D. Mabbot's *The State and the Citizen* (which Liddington cites but fails to follow consistently the implications of). In this review, Oakeshott is critical of Mabbot's claim that an individual self's relations with others may "determine what it does, but not what it is" (Oakeshott, 2007, p. 255). Oakeshott goes on to give the Idealist view that the individual is defined by its relations with social whole, but it is Oakeshott's discussion of the relation of different levels of analysis which is of concern here:

> Now that this "individual" is something observable at ground level no one will doubt... The "private individual" as I understand him is a social... a legal, creation... Nothing is more certain than that this individual would collapse, like a body in a vacuum, if he were removed from the "external" social world which is the condition of his existence... *And further, the "individual" who is visible at ground level may have a different appearance when we have ascended the tower, and... the whole notion of man as one among others may dissolve...* But... it would be a disaster if on our return to ground level we should attempt to apply what we had seen from the top... (*ibid.*, pp. 255–256, emphasis added)

Let us turn now to review some instances where Liddington does not seem to observe that Oakeshott has shifted the level of analysis to the more comprehensive or more general, starting with his criticisms of Oakeshott's account of experience and its modalities, and moving onto

Oakeshott's account of the modern state as subsisting in a tension between two ideal types of association. While I do not think this move can account for all their differences, it can account for the most important ones in my view.

Liddington is critical of Oakeshott's account of the historical modality of experience on the grounds that it is simply false, in particular with regard to two claims. The *first* is Oakeshott's claim that the character of historical events is *exhausted* in their relations, and the *second*, that the *sole* criterion of historical truth is coherence (among relations of historical events) (Liddington, 1985, pp. 52–58). For (the realist) Liddington, the ultimate criterion of history is correspondence to the evidence of the past. For Liddington, "to demand that the historical past be absolutely present is to demand that it cease to exist." "It is dependent on the present but is not itself the present" (*ibid.*, p. 88). Yet, in Oakeshott's more general and comprehensive perspective, all coherent experience is always a present "world" of ideas. This is both definitional and arguably accurate. Even personal memories exist only in present experience. On Oakeshott's creativist account both the practical and historical past exist in a present world of ideas, and are created by, or "are correlative to", the mediating principle which enables them to escape nonentity by giving them a distinctive, recognizable and characteristic shape. The *coherence* of the historical world of experience for Oakeshott demands that it meet Liddington's requirement that "it *correspond* to the evidence of the past", if it is to be coherent in the sense that it is "obliged" to take into account the latest, best available evidence from the relevant past. It thus escapes Liddington's criticism in this regard, in my view.

Liddington's critiques of Oakeshott's account of the scientific modality of experience follows the same script — since the coherence theory of truth can apply only to analytic or deductive systems, Oakeshott cannot account for the empirical side of the activity of science, and errs in treating all non-analytic scientific conclusions as merely statistical generalizations. Yet, again, Liddington appears not to appreciate the high level of generality at which Oakeshott's exposition functions. For Oakeshott "science" is the mediation of experience on the principle of quantity (and stability and communicability), and creates its own subject matter as do all sustained modifications of experience. When Liddington argues that Oakeshott still relies in part on the correspondence theory of knowledge and truth, he is *almost* correct, except that the *correspondence* is not between a "something merely out there"[5] and the mind, but between the latest evidence (scientifically defined) and theories about it, without which correspondence scientific experience would diminish in coherence. If Einstein's theories about the curvature of time and space, for example, had not been confirmed by contemporary measurements not available to him, his theories would have been rejected in that regard by the scientific community, and this, on Oakeshott's usage, is a matter of coherence; that is, accommodation within an interderpendent system of identical parts to one another's claims. In the same fashion, Oakeshott would have also called a matter of increasing coherence the way in which Einstein's theories were made compatible with Newton's laws by observing that the latter were still valid for matter subject to relatively low levels of gravitational pull and moving at speeds well below that of light.

Liddington's critique of Oakeshott's account of practical experience (the world of value and will) is similar to, but more expansive than, his critiques of Oakeshott on history and science. It argues that Oakeshott fails to show that the "world" (a system of mutually dependent parts) of practice is coherent in any appreciable degree, and is in fact a self-contradictory account (Liddington, 1985, p. 144). On Liddington's view, Oakeshott's description of practical action to reconcile or bridge the gap between "what is" and "what ought to be" violates the requirement that experience be always present, not *future*, experience. Yet, again, this critique does not consider that "what ought to be" is also a *present* idea for Oakeshott just as is the historical *past*. In my view, then, this criticism of Oakeshott's account of practical experience misses the mark.

Liddington has, however, another general criticism of Oakeshott's account of practical experience, which he also directs to Oakeshott's account of historical and scientific experience. This is his claim that a modality of experience cannot contain its own presuppositions:

> His mistake is to suppose that the practical world as a whole can contain *both* practical activity *and* the presuppositions of that activity. *This is a mistake because an experience and its presuppositions cannot belong to the same world... Presuppositions are not in way dependent on that which presupposes them.* (ibid., pp. 142–143, emphasis added)

Now, this is an interesting claim, although in my opinion it is more *apropos* as a criticism of Oakeshott's account of practice than of history and science, since the latter two are intellectual disciplines which are explicit about the criteria which shall be taken into account in deciding

---

5   "...when we speak of *it* our language slips under our feet, for there is never in experience an *it*..." (Oakeshott, 1933, p. 31).

whether an assertion is "scientific" or "historical" (and this in spite of Oakeshott's hyperbolic claim that modes of experience cannot modify their presuppositions — Oakeshott, 1933, p. 282). Liddington's point here is that the presuppositions of a modality (e.g. contiguity, quantity, value) are not mutually dependent on the world which they help to create, and that since "what is" and "what ought to be" are different worlds of experience, bridging from one to another denies their character as separate worlds of experience. Since I have argued that they are both the same present world of experience, I do not see that this charge lands, though I do think that Liddington is persuasive here in offering a more satisfactory account of Oakeshott's idea of practical action by saying that it conceives "practical activity as the attempt to enhance the coherence of a single world: the present practical world of value" (Liddington, 1985, p. 153). It should be clear by now that Liddington's general critique of Oakeshott's account of both experience and philosophical experience (the investigation of presuppositions *ad infinitum*) is that by reducing "the Absolute" to an implied, coherent, timeless idea[6] it risks sliding into a highly subjective and intuitive kind of "temporal solipsism", but as I follow Oakeshott the philosophic obligation to investigate and resolve the contradictions in the best available evidence in any modality acts as a bulwark against this kind of solipsism (as does the later Daoist-like emphasis on practical skill in his critique of modern rationalism[7]).

Of Liddington's many (often minute) criticisms of Oakeshott's account of experience, two more may be of general interest. The first is his claim that Oakeshott's account of individuality in the practical modality amounts to nonentity and contradicts the character of all experience as a world of ideas. His point here is that Oakeshott's account of the practical self as "separate, unique and self-contained" and "ungoverned by relations" contradicts Oakeshott's claim that whatever is "without relations must be devoid of significance and

---

[6] It is definitional for Oakeshott in *Experience and Its Modes* that truth, reality, and knowledge are one and the same coherent world of experience and that this postulated coherent world does not exist in the future, but is logically implied as a sort of eternal presence (Oakeshott, 1933, pp. 35, 263). However, Liddington is understandably concerned that reality may not be the same as truth (or logical self-sufficiency or coherence). And if the criterion for what is completely satisfactory in experience is *neither* a present nor future world of ideas, *but rather* an *always* implied world of ideas, then, in my view, one might reasonably wonder if Oakeshott has, or has not, corrected Kant's insulation of ultimate reality from theoretical reason.

[7] For development of this theme, see Coats and Cheung (2012).

consequently falls outside of experience" (Liddington, 1985, p. 155). Liddington then summarizes his characterization of Oakeshott here:

> In short, instead of a homogeneous world of intrinsically related and mutually dependent individuals, Oakeshott offers us a chaos of isolated self-determined individuals. (*ibid.*, p. 156)

And, Liddington even cites instances written both before and after *Experience and Its Modes* (1933), where Oakeshott gives an account of individuality more consistent with his view of coherence in experience, even citing the Mabbot review which was discussed above. Yet Oakeshott is explicit in that review that the philosophic view of the individual as defined by relations with others is not the designated conventional and legal individual "at ground level", and that it is an error to attempt to bring philosophic insights directly into practical discourse (except perhaps as a limitation on it). It is clear in this instance that Oakeshott is describing the presuppositions of the practical self as he conceives it, and that while the practical self may lack the degree of coherence of philosophic experience it as least has sufficient coherence to escape "nonentity".

The issue of degrees of coherence touches on a related criticism Liddington makes of Oakeshott's account of the modaties of experience. This is his claim that it is a logical error to attempt to define distinct modalities of experience without establishing their *degree* of coherence but that Oakeshott does not wish to attempt this because it would suggest that a modality with a higher degree of coherence (e.g. science) should have competence in a less coherent modality (e.g. practice), and that philosophy as the most coherent form of experience should have competence in (rather than merely supersede) less coherent forms of experience (Liddington, 1985, pp. 178–179). Now, Oakeshott himself suggests that while it may be hypothetically possible to establish degrees of coherence, it may also be beyond the capacity of human intellect to do so. An alternative, which neither suggests, is that it might be possible to establish a minimum threshold of coherence necessary for a distinct modality of experience to escape "nonentity", which I think is what Oakeshott does by implication in his expositions of the modalities of experience.

Liddington turns next to a brief discussion of Oakeshott's criticisms of modern rationalism in his essays of the 1940s and 1950s, collected in *Rationalism in Politics*. He analyses critically Oakeshott's distinction between technical knowledge which can be formulated and put in books, and practical knowledge (of timing and degree of action) which is more general and cannot be satisfactorily formulated in propositions but is learned in apprenticeship; and Oakeshott's criticism of rationalist ideologies and moralities for their destruction of genuine skill and moral balance of established crafts, professions, and social, political, and religious traditions. He notes (correctly I think) that traditions for Oakeshott are worlds of experience (in the language of *Experience and Its Modes*), that is, evolved systems of mutually dependent parts unsusceptible to the distinction between essence and accident or existence, in which (like a dry stone wall) no one element is more essential than another.

Liddington's main criticism of Oakeshott in this connection (based on slight differences in the various essays) is that Oakeshott is uncertain about the place of reflective intellect in practical and moral life, and whether an ideology is an abridgement of a tradition or can be conceived independent of one (Liddington, 1985 p. 205). Yet, I think, Oakeshott's final position on this (in the 1949 essay "The Tower of Babel") is clear enough: the proper role of reflective intellect in living moral, political, and religious practices is as critic, not instigator, of action; and as protector of the traditions (from which they evolve) during times of crisis and upheaval. In my view, this is a sound argument also supported by many philosophers and social theorists – the *explicit* is always weaker and more susceptible to attack than the *implicit*, but is also needed when a living tradition or practice is under attack, especially by a rationalist ideology.[8]

In the last section of his thesis Liddington is concerned to show the failure of Oakeshott's account in *On Human Conduct* (1975) of the modern European state as embodying a tension between what

---

[8] Liddington characteristically argues here that Oakeshott's idea of practical knowledge (how) is more susceptible to explanation as *coherence* than his idea of technical knowledge (that, what), which is better explained by the correspondence theory of truth, because practical knowledge lacks a pre-determined end. Yet, again, this distinction is also one of degree of generality in my view. As an end becomes more general (e.g. security, peace, moral virtue) it specifies no specific actions except coherence among a complex of ideas. Even a technical craft such as pottery requires coherence among its mutually dependent practical and technical parts if it is to be skilful. In different ways the coherence and correspondence theories of truth both attempt to recapture the connection to reality of the pre-nominalist Aristotelian claim in *De Anima* that the beings of the world are in soul (*psyche*) and that knowing is intellective conjunction with the "beings that are". The coherence theory does this by beginning from the "whole" of which something less than the whole is predicated in assertions and actions; the correspondence theory by trying to bridge the nominalist gap between *ideas* of the mind and the *things* of the world. Yet, as I have argued throughout, the coherence theory is the more comprehensive of the two, and better able to accommodate the concerns of the other.

Oakeshott calls "civil association" and "enterprise (or purposive) association". In essence Liddington argues that this account fails because neither of the ideal types approximates anything in actual experience. As I have said, in my view, the controversy between Liddington and Oakeshott is exacerbated by Oakeshott's recurrent and mischievous employment of the literary trope of hyperbole, and by his typical expository method of describing two qualitatively different ideal types or logical constructs, as contrasted with the view that they are points of degree on a continuum. I shall try to show how Oakeshott's meaning here can be made clearer, and then use my reconstruction of Oakeshott's argument to reply to Liddington's central objections. At issue here will be the meaning of Oakeshott's undefined terms, such as "general purpose" or "concern", "substantive purpose", instrumental", "non-instrumental", "prudential", and "moral". My view, as will become apparent, is that the distinction in the meaning of all these terms can be explained in terms of increasing and decreasing degrees of generality, and that (as I have argued elsewhere[9]) Oakeshott's account of freedom under general laws follows intellectual moves similar to those Rousseau used in describing law as the expression of the general will.

This mature work, *On Human Conduct*, consists of three long, related essays. The first delineates a theoretical perspective on human activity Oakeshott calls "human conduct", understood as intelligent (or not so intelligent) activity requiring learning and choice, and also a method within that perspective for "theorizing" a performance within conduct which he calls "theorizing contingency". This sounds like Oakeshott's earlier account of writing history, that is, telling a story with no beginning and no end, in which explanation is based upon contiguity between what went before and what came after. Oakeshott distinguishes this perspective from "covering law" explanations (such as those of social science) and says it is the only way of explaining an event in human conduct "without explaining it away" as does social science in importing a foreign, causal explanatory principle. The second essay delineates a form of association which Oakeshott calls "civil" and distinguishes it from another form of association which Oakeshott calls "enterprise" or purposive association. (These are pure types or logical constructs to aid in understanding.) The third essay in *On Human Conduct* offers a lengthy account of a modern European state as evolving in the historical fortunes of interaction between those who thought of a state as a very general civil association, and those who conceived it a more specific, purposive association—we might say, in

---

[9]   See Coats (2000, pp. 76–88).

an abbreviated way, between those who thought of the state in a *civil* Roman way, and then who thought of the state in a *political* Greek way.[10]

In this exposition Oakeshott uses pairs of terms (largely undefined) whose meaning has to be deduced from the way they are employed in specific contexts, terms such as formal—substantive, moral—prudential, instrumental—non-instrumental, authority—power, among others. In my view, and as I shall try to show, the difference in Oakeshott's often idiosyncratic usage can be satisfactorily explained as a matter of increasing or decreasing generality, and rephrasing Oakeshott's exposition in this fashion will allow it to escape Liddington's major criticisms of it.

Oakeshott's account of the ideal type "civil association" is meant to depict the features of a compulsory association which can preserve the widest possible latitude for individual choice to maintain the link between belief and conduct. His fundamental point here as I understand him is that the more *general* the terms of association, the more latitude for individual choice in private pursuits. Thus, he sometimes says that civil association does *not* have a purpose, or a substantive purpose, such as alleviation of the condition of the poor, for that would enlist all participants and activities in that pursuit. Yet, it also becomes clear in his usage that he observes the difference *between* a general purpose or "concern" such as security, peace, *tranquillitas*, moral virtue, *and* a *substantive* purpose such as getting in the harvest or putting out fires (Oakeshott, 1975, p. 49). The differences in the two kinds of purpose is that (1) a *general* purpose prescribes no particular actions unambiguously (does providing for the common defence mean military conscription or not?), and (2) a *general* purpose is not exhausted in any particular action but persists throughout the activity. A *substantive* purpose, by contrast, in Oakeshott's usage (1) can be more precisely and unambiguously stipulated and visibly identified, (2) is exhausted in being accomplished, and (3) leaves little freedom of choice in its accomplishment (although even here there can be some small ambiguity—is getting in 85 percent of the harvest the same as "getting in the harvest?"). Thus when critics such as Liddington argue that Oakeshott is mistaken when he says hyperbolically on occasion that civil association (*versus* enterprise association) has no purpose, it is clear enough I think that he means it has no *substantive* purpose.

Another controversial feature of Oakeshott's account of civil association is his claim that civil association is *moral* (*vs.* prudential) association, where morality is understood to mean the general and

---

[10] For this theme, see the fifth essay of this collection.

formal procedural ways in which specific actions are qualified. (Liddington in particular quarrels with Oakeshott's view that morality is not a matter of *substantive* actions.) Yet if we look at Oakeshott's implied definitions of these terms it is clear enough what he means, perhaps building on Aristotle's observation that action is always specific. Constitutive law by its very general nature does not prohibit specific actions, but rather the procedures and context within which they are taken. Laws prohibit *not* killing or lighting fires, but killing murderously or lighting fires arsonously, for example.

Morality, for Oakeshott, only arises in a general context, and this is also his reason for contrasting "moral" with "prudential" and "instrumental". The issue again has to do with increasing and decreasing levels of generality. When Oakeshott says, again hyperbolically, that moral practices are not "prudential" or instrumental for the accomplishment of patterns of desired outcomes, he would appear to mean that moral conditions are by their very nature so generally stipulated that, most of the time, they stipulate no *unambiguously* specific actions (even lying may be qualified on moral grounds in matters of natural security). And when Liddington complains that the very existence of language is meant to enhance the purpose of furthering communication, he certainly has a point, but Oakeshott would reply that furthering communication is a *general* concern or purpose, and not a *substantive*, unambiguously achieved one, observable in action. (In making his objection, Liddington likes to focus on "borderline" cases—is, for example, "killing brutally" a substantive action or a procedurally qualified one?)

Similarly, when Oakeshott says that the ideal type, civil association, is not instrumental for, or is indifferent to, the accomplishment of purposes, this clearly does not refer to *general* purposes or concerns such as the ones he enumerates—security, peace, moral virtue, etc. And, the same kind of analysis can be applied to Oakeshott's strict separation of legitimate authority and mere power, and his observation that it takes a rare and disciplined civic imagination to enact and maintain it in practice. Yet at a certain level of generality, the distinction is not so clear. Every constitutional shape (as Aristotle observed in his taxonomy of regimes) makes a claim about justice, and justice is partially a matter of power. At times it is difficult not to suspect that Oakeshott invites being misunderstood, although it is not clear whether from a mischievous playfulness or as a rhetorical and pedagogic technique to further understanding.

I have tried in this essay to respond to Liddington's criticisms of Oakeshott's various themes because they are among the deepest ones I know of made by someone who undertook to understand Oakeshott in detail, and they merit careful examination. To rehearse, I have tried to show that Liddington's concern that Oakeshott's account of experience (based on a coherence theory of truth) is in danger of sliding into solipsism and post-modernist subjectivism is misplaced because Oakeshott's account subsumes the concerns of the correspondence theory of truth and not the other way around. Secondly, I have argued that in his essays on modern rationalism Oakeshott is not uncertain on the role of reflective intellect in balanced and skilful moral, political, and religious practices; rather, his final position is that it should be as critic, not instigator, of action, except in times of crisis. And, lastly, that Oakeshott's "bi-form" account of the modern European state in *On Human Conduct* does not "fail" (as Liddington would have it), if Oakeshott's understanding of the terms "purpose", "moral", "prudential", and "instrumental" are understood in terms of increasing and decreasing levels of generality, respectively.

To conclude on a positive (although "un-Oakeshottian") note, the *utility* of Oakeshott's account of difference and plurality as *modalities* of experience as a whole, which nonetheless have no direct competence for one another, lies arguably in its focus on the centrality of the logical error of irrelevance (*ignoratio elenchi*) involved when philosophy, history, science, practice, and art try to carry their conclusions into one another's respective realms. The result, as Oakeshott observes in his essays of the 1940s and 1950s is loss of skill and balance. And although Oakeshott restricts science to its own realm, his account of experience rejects specifiable degrees of reality (beyond mere nonentity) and supports the medieval creative insight which fractured the teleological worldview (and its view of degrees of being), and made possible modern empirical science[11] — hardly a post-modernist development.

References

Coats, W.J. Jr (2000) *Oakeshott and His Contemporaries*, London: Associated University Presses.

Coats, W.J. Jr. & Cheung, C.-Y. (2012) *The Poetic Character of Human Activity*, Lanham, MD: Lexington Books.

Foster, M.B. (1934) "The Christian Doctrine of Creation and the Rise of Modern Natural Science", *Mind*, Vol. 43 (Oct).

Liddington, J. (1985) *The Philosophy of Michael Oakeshott and its Relation to Politics*, doctoral thesis, Balliol College, Oxford University, photocopy.

Liddington, J. (1984) "Oakeshott: Freedom in a Modern European State", in Gray, J. & Pelczyuski, Z. (eds.) *Conceptions of Liberty in Political Philosophy*, London: Athlone Press.

---

[11] For this theme, see Foster (1934).

Oakeshott, M.J. (1933) *Experience and Its Modes*, Cambridge: Cambridge University Press.

Oakeshott, M.J. (1975) *On Human Conduct*, Oxford: Clarendon Press.

Oakeshott, M.J. (1962) *Rationalism in Politics and Other Essays*, London: Methuen and Co., Ltd.

Oakeshott, M.J. (2007) "Review of *The State and The Citizen* by J.D. Mabbot", in O'Sullivan, L. (ed.) *The Concept of a Philosophical Jurispondence*, Exeter: Imprint Academic.

Seven

Practical Implications of Learning for its Own Sake

An Attempt at Synthesis of Oakeshott and Whitehead on University Education

"Intellect could be concerned with the soul, with the cosmos, as it was for so long… It has concerned itself with temporal life, with politics in the broad sense. The more it is concerned with politics, the more irresponsible it becomes." — Charles de Gaulle, 1969.

In his 1934 review of Whitehead's *Adventures of Ideas* (Oakeshott, 2007), Oakeshott characterized Whitehead's style in that book and others as often vague and obscure, but also peppered with brilliant insights. (He also professed rhetorically not to understand Whitehead's philosophical views, especially as set forth in the difficult book *Process and Reality*.) For anyone who has read some of Whitehead's works, these characterizations must seem apt, both with regard to his popular as well as philosophic and scientific writing. Nevertheless, I believe it is both possible and profitable to compare and contrast with Oakeshott's some of Whitehead's more lucid views on the life and education of the mind, as found in some lectures he gave at Harvard and Princeton in the late 1920s and as collected in two separate books, *The Aims of Education and Other Essays*, and *The Function of Reason*.

There are many obstacles to this comparison. Alfred North Whitehead, a philosopher of science, and a generation Oakeshott's senior, was a rationalist who believed in civilized Progress, and who wrote and thought within what Oakeshott would call the practical past, present, and future. Nevertheless, and in spite of a Teutonic-like tendency for obscure renderings, Whitehead's intellect could be subtle, imaginative, and self-critical. He was especially critical, for example, of dogmatic scientific rationalism for its failure to incorporate the insights of what he called creativity, and more generally of any established doctrine or methodology which had outgrown its usefulness, i.e. no longer provided balance for the processional flux of reality.

At any rate, I propose in these remarks to "bracket" Whitehead's obscure "process philosophy" (which Oakeshott professed not to understand, but which arguably has similarities to Oakeshott's idea of the poetic character of human activity), and focus here on some of his popular views on the functions of education and speculative reason in the life of civilizations. Oakeshott and Whitehead were both talented and perceptive teachers, imaginatively alive to what was occurring around them, and both were especially concerned with the twentieth-century pedagogic tendency to focus increasingly on instrumental outcomes to the exclusion of other concerns. However, and to anticipate myself a bit, their criticisms of the focus on narrow instrumentality in pedagogy took different turns—both lauded learning and understanding for its own sake, but for different reasons. In the case of Whitehead, for its ultimate contribution to civilized progress; in the case of Oakeshott the reason is more complex, as we shall see. I'll proceed by laying on the relevant views of each on the subject then see where they may overlap and support one another, *malgré tout*.

Let us begin with Whitehead's views on the aims of university education by looking in some detail at an uncharacteristically lucid address he delivered at Harvard University in 1928, on the occasion of its incorporating a school of business. In this address, entitled "Universities and their Function", Whitehead develops the following themes.

He notes that the expansion of universities in the developed world, and especially America, may present a danger by destroying the usefulness of universities, if there is not widespread understanding of the primary functions which universities should perform in the service of a nation. To illustrate his general point, he chooses the case of the newly founded business school at Harvard University, "a new fact in the university world" (in spite of universities having trained kings, clerks, clergy, doctors, lawyers, and engineers over the past seven hundred years) (Whitehead, 1929a, p. 138). However, since the curriculum for business schools is still in an experimental stage (in 1928) some recurrence to general principles of university education is called for in moulding that curriculum. What are these general principles?

Whitehead begins his account of the proper function of universities by noting that although they are both schools of education and schools of research, the primary reason for universities is to be found in neither function, both of which could be performed at a cheaper rate outside the university. Rather,

> the justification for a university is that it preserves the connection between knowledge and the zest for life, by uniting the young and the old in the imaginative consideration of learning. (*ibid.*, p. 139)

And although a university does impart knowledge, it does so imaginatively, and, if not, has no reason for existence. By generating an atmosphere of excitement, knowledge is transformed from prosaic facts into energizing possibilities. Such knowledge, far from burdening the memory, energizes us as "the poet of our dreams, and as the architect of our purposes", and enables the construction of an "intellectual vision of the world" which can consider alternative possibilities to the *status quo*. Recognizing that the energy of youthful imagination is strengthened by discipline, the university seeks "to weld together imagination and experience" (*ibid.*, p. 140).

Yet the initial discipline of imagination requires that "there be no responsibility for immediate action". The capacity of eliciting illustrations of general principles in unbiased thought "cannot be acquired when there is the daily task of preserving a concrete organization: you must be free... to appreciate the variousness of the universe undisturbed by its perils". Whitehead next goes on to apply these general reflections on the historically evolved functions of the university. This means first that the function of a business school is to produce individuals with a zest for life and business: "It is a libel upon human nature to conceive that zest for life is the product of pedestrian purposes directed toward the narrow routine of material comforts. But in modern, social complexities the adventure of life cannot be disjoined from intellectual adventure." Today business organization requires an imaginative grasp of psychology, geography, sociology, economics, political science, public administration, health and hygiene, diplomacy, applied science, and "a sympathetic vision of the limits of human nature and of the conditions which evoke loyalty of service" (*ibid.*, pp. 141–142). All of this is intended to promote the imaginative consideration of the general principles underlying business or any other career. For Whitehead, then, the proper function and utility of a university is the imaginative acquisition of knowledge — apart from this, "there is no reason why businessmen, and other professional men should not pick up their facts bit by bit if they want them..." (*ibid.*, p. 145).

He then takes up *imagination* and how it is sustained. It can only be communicated by a faculty "who wear their learning with imagination", as symbolized by the ancient image of a torch being passed from hand to hand across generations (*ibid.*, p. 145). For Whitehead, the lighted torch represents the imagination of which he is speaking. And it is here that the danger arises in the recent extension in number of university students and variety of university activities — the problem must not be mishandled. In order to combine imagination and learning, an entire way of life must be cultivated in the university which provides leisure, freedom from worry, and self-confidence, deriving from "pride in the achievements of the surrounding society in procuring the advance of knowledge" (*ibid.*, p. 146). Imagination cannot be kept in "an ice box and produced periodically in stated quantities" (*ibid.*, p. 146). The solution here is to combine teaching with research. Teachers are kept imaginative by engaging in research, and researchers are kept imaginative by explaining their research to eager, imaginative young minds, who in turn will profit by contact "with minds softened with experience of intellectual adventure". In fact, "...the universities should be homes of adventure shared in common by young and old" (*ibid.*, p. 147), and one way of keeping alive this spirit of adventure is by making knowledge fresh for the young. On Whitehead's view, the function of scholars as a whole for a professive society is to "evoke into life wisdom and beauty which, apart from their magic, would remain lost in the past"; and this is the mechanism provided through the university such that "study may influence the market place, and the market place the study" (*ibid.*, p. 148).

Whitehead also explicitly cautions here against treating the management of a university faculty as analogous to that of a business organization, for the heart of university activity "lies beyond all regulation, and the attempt to regulate it in the manner of a business corporation will only succeed in producing a faculty of very efficient pedants and dullards", something the general public may not discern until years of stunted growth for promising youth. "The faculty should be a brand of scholars stimulating each other, and freely determining their various activities" (*ibid.*, p. 149).

Let us pass from Whitehead's remarks on the proper function of universities, to a series of lectures on the function of reason given at Princeton University at about the same time. Our aim here is to integrate Whitehead's view on the proper function of universities with his broader view of the biological function of reason in human evolution. These lectures, comprising some seventy-odd pages, are also surprisingly lucid and accessible (for Whitehead's writing). To anticipate momentarily, it turns out that the biological function of *speculative* reason is to provide enough order (through disciplined logical analysis) for the anarchic, human creative impulse toward novelty to rescue it from chaos. In so doing it thereby insulates a civilized way of life against the rhythmic, natural tendency from growth to decay, enabling it to progress toward higher levels of generalized insight. Let us look at some of the details of Whitehead's exposition of this theme.

Whitehead begins by distinguishing practical reason from speculative reason, the former evolving over millions of years, the latter only without the last two (or three if we count non-mathematical Asian speculation) thousand years. Reason itself evolves to contain and discriminate among the novelties introduced by higher human mental appetitions, and, thereby, rescues them from anarchy. But practical reason, functioning at a lower level, is primarily concerned with establishing pragmatic techniques and methods with "a short range of forecast", and little foresight to break out of the natural rhythm of growth and decay. Speculative reason (which Whitehead sometimes calls Platonic) seeks understanding and explanation for its own sake as one of the elements of the good life, but, in seeking understanding for its own sake, also eventually begins to better practical and productive life, by introducing disciplined novelty to contain and break free from the rhythm of natural decay. Decay arises when the practical techniques initially embodied in human institutions fail to deal adequately with the new and the changing:

> It is surprising that a scheme of such abstract ideas [as mathematical physics] should have proved to be of such importance. We can imagine that an Egyptian country gentlemen at the beginning of the Greek period might have tolerated the technical devices of his land surveyors, but would have felt the airy generalizations of the speculative Greeks were tenuous, unpractical, waste of time. The obscurantists of all ages exhibit the same principles. All common sense is with them. Their only serious antagonist is History and the history of Europe is dead against them. Abstract speculation has been the salvation of the world — speculations which made systems and then transcended them, speculations which ventured to the furthest lists of abstraction. To set limits to speculation is treason to the future. (1929b, p. 60)

To link up, then, Whitehead's themes on the functions of university education with those of the functions of reason, we might say that the social function of universities for him is to create and sustain an institutionalized environment conducive to creative speculation for its own sake, thereby simultaneously generating the practical and material conditions for its own escape (for a while longer) from the rhythmic cycle of decay in all things.

Now, how do Whitehead's reflections in this connection parallel and contrast with Oakeshott's? In attempting an answer to this, I'll draw upon those of Oakeshott's educational essays collected in Tim Fuller's *The Voice of Liberal Learning* and Luke O'Sullivan's *What is History and Other Essays*, against the backdrop of Oakeshott's broader philosophic concerns. Oakeshott shares a number of broad themes with Whitehead and, as Efraim Podoksik has documented, Oakeshott's own, independent articulation of these themes was influential in British educational debates in the second half of the twentieth century (Podoksik, 2003, pp. 224–229).

These common themes include concerns over the reduction of education from the transmission of a civilized inheritance across generations *to* a set of instrumental techniques for attainment of specific, substantive purposes; and a defence of learning and understanding for its own sake, released for a while from the anxiety of satisfying material wants and competing for status. Rather than rehearse Oakeshott's well-known account (at least to this readership) of "the voice of liberal learning", I'd like instead to illustrate these broader themes by turning in some detail to a less known talk from Oakeshott's papers given to a group of entering LSE students around 1960 and entitled "On Arriving at a University" (included in Luke O'Sullivan's collection *What is History?*). This entertaining little talk is full of rhetorical tropes designed to evoke laughter and relaxation in the listeners (for instance, "you came here to learn to be a productive member of society — forget it") (Oakeshott, 2004, p. 334). But when his tone begins to wax more serious, Oakeshott gives a brief, lucid account in different words of why a place of learning is a "place apart". He tells these first year undergraduates that they are at university because the "inventers of it (whoever they were) seem to have thought it a good thing, even for people who are going to spend their lives in practical occupations... to get acquainted with the 'academic' attitude to things". He then proceeds to explain to them what is the "academic" attitude, and its relation, such as it is, to practical life:

> It is a peculiar attitude... the value of which does not depend upon its immediate usefulness in practical life; indeed, it can be said to have no more than an oblique bearing upon practical life. (*ibid.*, p. 337)

> The positive side of being 'academic' is being concerned, not with... merely how things work and what they can be used for, but *with explanations*. (*ibid.*, p. 337)

And explanation and understanding in turn require leisure or release from "the necessity of doing anything or learning how to do anything". Oakeshott then explains the difference between the "doer" (which is most folks for most of their lives) and the "academic explainer". For the "doer", the world is material to be conquered, exploited, and made use of. For the explainer, the world is something to be understood, not used; to be made intelligible, not exploited (*ibid.*, p. 338).

Oakeshott then goes on to characterize, for these LSE under-graduates, the meaning of the murky phrase the "social sciences". These studies he says are "concerned with different kinds of explana-tions of human conduct". These kinds of explanations are not fixed and are not in conflict with one another. He briefly characterizes three — Economics, History, and Politics. Economics tries to explain conduct from the standpoint of making choices "between courses of action"; it is not about knowing what to do — it is a 'world of explanatory, not practical, ideas". History, similarly, is making conduct intelligible from its own peculiar standpoint (which we know from other of Oakeshott's works is the study of the past for its own sake). And, Politics is the study of the activity of governing and being governed from a compre-hensive standpoint encompassing "historical, legal, psychological, and philosophical explanations". And Oakeshott concludes this little address by reminding these beginning university students that, while they may acquire some useful information over the next three years, they are at university primarily to get practice in thinking in ways "in which an economist or a historican or a mathematician or a philosopher thinks. And you are here to get some practice in expressing your thoughts" (*ibid.*, pp. 338–339).

Now, what overlap or coincidence do we find in the views on the modern dangers to university life of these two different thinkers, the imaginative scientific rationalist and the imaginative philosophic skeptic (who "would do better if he only knew how")? In my view, and in spite of their deeper differences over the whole idea of cumulative, civilized progress, both share a rather similar view of the functioning of institutions of higher learning. Both see places of higher learning as "places apart", places of leisure insulated from the concern for immediate practical results, and places the historically evolved, institu-tionally embodied ambience of which is threatened by the outside world's increasing demands on it for immediate results relevant to the satisfaction of its wants and felt needs. Both thinkers imply that this demand may issue in a reduction in scope of the imagination of the educated of our species, evident in a new university emphasis on training in relevant techniques, rather than in transmission across generations of generalized, tacit knowledge even within specified academic disciplines. The biggest difference between our two thinkers is Whithead's unwavering conviction that insulated places for unfettered and unrestrained speculation will issue in a cumulative progress in using the world's resources, which can resist the natural cycle of decay. Whitehead thus provides a long-range utilitarian defence of a short-range non-utilitarian view of university education, a project about which Oakeshott (for whom the world in general has no meaning) is far more skeptical. Oakeshott's reasons for defending his university traditions against the Rationalist post-war onslaught were, arguably, both moral and aesthetic. "Moral" in the sense of the view set out in his 1948 essay, "The Tower of Babel", in which the proper role of critical intellect in a balanced moral tradition is to protect it in times of crisis, which Oakeshott was attempting in his educational essays (including "Rationalism in Politics"); "aesthetic" in the sense that this tradition was his own (in this he was a believer, not a critical skeptic); that he had come to enjoy it; and that he wished to keep it.

In attempting, by way of some concluding remarks, to mediate between the views on higher education of these two most perceptive thinkers, let me suggest the following. While both are concerned to preserve the historically evolved, institutional life of English universities and colleges as they inherited it in the first half of the twentieth century, there is clearly a greater emphasis in Whitehead on the long-range practical consequences of this "non-consequentialist" pedagogy. Yet, some of this difference in emphasis derives from Oakeshott's characteristic way of writing and expositing in all his works. In general, we might characterize it as following an Helegian pattern for progressing logically from understanding (*Verstand,* dealing with contradictions) to reason (*Vernunft,* resolution of contradictions in the study of any subject matter). In the tradition of philosophic idealism, this method is based on "the identity of identity and non-identity". Oakeshott's characteristic approach in any subject matter is to delineate two ideal types (e.g. civil *vs.* enterprise association, the politics or faith *vs.* the politics of skepticism, the individual *vs.* the individual *manqué*), in order later to synthesize them or hold them in tension, in some fashion. Yet this method demands strict delineation of the contradictory ideals prior to either their synthesis, or managed polarity. In combination with Oakeshott's penchant for the rhetorical trope of hyperbole, this method of argument often leads to the insistence on categorical differences, which might from a different explanatory perspective be viewed as different points on a gradual continuum. For example, Oakeshott's well-known insistence on the difference between general and substantive (or instrumental) purposes in the context of law might be viewed as simply a difference in an ascending scale of generality, i.e. what Oakeshott calls a general purpose is simply a purpose that has become so general that it can no longer be visualized in discrete action (such as lighting a fire) but can only be specified in general adverbial terms (such as a prohibition on lighting a fire arsonously). In a similar manner, Oakeshott's insistence on the strict separation *between* explanation and understanding for its own sake *and* understanding how things work and how to use and "exploit" them can also be viewed on a scale of ascending or descending generality, as can the differences between consequentialist or utilitarian *versus* non-consequentialist moralities (recall here David Hume's Ciceronian argument in his treatise on morals that all enduring moral codes have embedded in them some functional utility). Understanding how something works and how to use it can, with certain minds, progress into understanding the grounds for its practical existence — in Plato's *Republic*, for example, one of the paths for ascent to comprehension of the "beings that are" was through mastery of a particular craft or profession so complete that one became interested in the structural similarities in all crafts and professions.

And even Oakeshott concedes, in brief asides, that categorical logical distinctions are abstractions from an ontological continuum, as when he tells the LSE undergraduates that the academic attitude toward value does not depend on something's *immediate* usefulness, and that it has only an *oblique* relation to practical life. (In other words the "academic attitude" has some relation to practical life, even if long-range and oblique.) Oakeshott's real criticism of twentieth-century pedagogy and politics in this context is not with utilitarian explanations *per se*, but with the unexamined faith that knowing how to do something constitutes an imperative to do it, a blindness which has evolved from a reduced moral consciousness, itself an evolution from the recent domination of the voice of practical experience in "the conversation of mankind". So, in an attempt at a brief concluding statement on Oakeshott and Whitehead on higher education, we might say that both were concerned to preserve (in the face of increasing demands for practical relevance) an inherited academic community and way of life nurturing generalists practised at speculative thought for its own sake, albeit with residual practical benefits.

References

Oakeshott, M.J. (2004) "On Arriving at a University", in O'Sullivan, L. (ed.) *What is History?*, pp. 337–339, Exeter: Imprint Academic.

Oakeshott, M.J. (2007) "Review of A.N. Whitehead, *Adventures of Ideas*", in O'Sullivan, L. 9ed.) *The Concept of a Philosophical Jurisprudence: Essays and Reviews*, pp. 73–75, Exeter: Imprint Academic.

Podoksik, E. (2003) *In Defence of Modernity*, pp. 224–229, Exeter: Imprint Academic.

Whitehead, A.N. (1929a) *The Aims of Education and Other Essays*, pp. 138–149, New York: The MacMillan Co.

Whitehead, A.N. (1929b) *The Function of Reason,* Princeton, NJ: Princeton University Press.

Eight

Politics, the Political, and Armed Force

Oakeshott, Schmitt, and Weber

This paper explores the relationship between the practice of politics and the resort to armed force and war in the thought of three twentieth-century thinkers—Michael Oakeshott, Carl Schmitt, and Max Weber. The choice of the two German thinkers in this investigation will appear obvious given the centrality of force in their respective definitions of politics, but why Oakeshott? In fact, the resort to war plays a central role in Oakeshott's historical reconstruction of the increasing prevalence of enterprise association and teleocratic conceptions of law and politics over civil association and nomocratic conceptions of law and politics.[1] The aim in this exploration is two-fold—both to use the resort to war in order to illuminate Oakeshott's characteristic expositional methods, as well as hopefully advance, just a bit, inquiry into the relationship of politics to war. The general drift of the paper's argument will be to suggest that how this relationship is conceived is definitively influenced by the methodological approach to the subject matter adopted by a thinker, an Oakeshottian insight apparent as far back as *Experience and Its Modes* (1933) where the distinction among modes of experience is grounded on the claim that they have no common subject matter since each creates its own in the distinctive way in which it mediates experience. And although this paper is primarily focused on the experience of the modern state, given the perennial nature of the question under investigation, it will also be found useful occasionally to refer back to the expositional method of Aristotle, who typically presents the "fullness" of any activity investigated, rather than focus solely on extreme cases and efficient causality, and whose approach is more closely approximated by Oakeshott than Schmitt,

---

[1]   For a detailed demonstration of this theme in Oakeshott's work, see Finn (2013, pp. 283–300).

Weber (or von Clausewitz). Let us begin in this connection with the views of Carl Schmitt, since of the three thinkers he gives the fullest account of the relationship between "the political" and the use of armed force by political authorities, even though he builds upon intellectual foundations laid by Max Weber.[2]

I. Schmitt

Although Schmitt's little book, *Der Begriff des Politischen*, appeared in three successively revised editions from 1927 to 1932 to indicate vulnerabilities of the German Weimar republic *vis-à-vis* extremist movements (as well as attempt to undermine the legitimacy of the Western Liberal ideology which grounded and imposed it), the heart of its argument about "the political" (not politics, *per se*) can be lifted from its historical context and independently evaluated, since it is very generally and abstractly stated and intends to make broad claims. Schmitt's is an infamous and controversial argument (especially given his later cooperation with the Nazi Party) but not one the details of which are generally known.

Schmitt's general way of arguing is to look at what is logically implied (and always has been implied) in the idea of "the political" and in political groupings. His main opponent is the Liberalism of the past two centuries which has gradually in his view replaced the primacy of the "political" with the primacy of "humanitarian ethics" on the one hand, and with technologically efficient and productive economic activity on the other. (It has thereby disguised its domination over others.)

On Schmitt's view political activity, by contrast, is defined by its extreme intensity, in particular in the capacity to make the final or sovereign decision for a group about when and against whom to go to war. In different words, political activity is deciding which groups (are "friends" and which) are public enemies against whom lethal force may be directed, and thus life within the group put at risk for some by others as part of the act of public defence. "By virtue of the power over the physical life of men, the political community transcends all other associations and societies" (1976, p. 47). On Schmitt's view, then, any grouping (e.g. a labour union) within an ostensibly political grouping which achieves this degree of intensity and influence (to make the final decision on the definition of public enemies) has become "political" in

---

2   See, in this context, Hennis (1988, p. 249). For important differences between Weber and Schmitt, especially over the issue of accommodation and reconciliation of opposing viewpoints as the stuff of politics, see Kelly (2003, pp. 159–160, 186) and Thornhill (2000, pp. 60–61).

lieu of the nominally governing authority, and one of the functions of political leadership is to prevent this occurring.

The portion of Schmitt's argument which requires careful analysis for our purposes, concerns the relationship of the "political" to war and the use of armed force. Schmitt distinguishes his view from that of the nineteenth-century theorist of war, von Clausewitz, by observing that for Clausewitz war is "a mere instrument of politics" (*ibid.*, p. 34). For Schmitt, however, the relationship is more subtle — it is the ever-present possibility of the extreme option of war which conditions behaviour we call "political", and, in fact, creates the political tension in a civilization:

> War is neither the aim nor the purpose nor even the very content of politics. *But as an ever present possibility it is the leading presupposition which determines in a characteristic way human action and thinking and thereby creates a specifically political behavior.* (*ibid.*, p. 34, emphasis added)

> What always matters is the possibility of the extreme case taking place... (*ibid.*, p. 35)

And, Schmitt argues that even where awareness of the "extreme case" has been lost, everyday language still retains the insight that politics is about fundamental antitheses which may have to be resolved by resort to armed force and war: "all political concepts... and terms have a polemical meaning" and turn into "ghostlike abstractions" when the possibility of the extreme case is denied (*ibid.*, p. 30). In brief, Schmitt is arguing that the essence of politics and the political is the capacity to order a community by making sovereign decisions about the definition of public enemies to the community (internal and external), and about the resort to use of lethal armed force to combat them if necessary. And, more broadly, that the essence of the "political" is definition and management of enmity, the reason why all political concepts have a polemical meaning.

Let us put aside Schmitt's argument against Liberalism and focus on his claims about the "political" and the resort to war. (Leo Strauss argued in a contemporary review of Schmitt's thesis that Schmitt had not in fact transcended "apolitical" liberalism because his implied criticism of it was a moral, not political, one — that is, that Liberalism's failure to focus on the "extreme case" meant that it was not "serious" and ignored or denied the "real order of things".[3] One might also

---

3   Strauss (1976, p. 99). For an attempt to demonstrate (based on his entire corpus) that Schmitt's overriding goal (in making the friend–enemy distinction the basis of the political) was to preserve the need for a decision between Christ and "the empire of the Antichrist" in a globally pacified world without politics, see Meier (2005, especially pp. 47–49). Another way of approaching this issue might be to say that Schmitt's criticism of

observe in this context that another feature which Schmitt's entire orientation shares with Lockean Liberalism is that for both Schmitt and Locke the "political" arises in the act upon life and property of others.)

From the standpoint of the meaning of politics and the political, Schmitt's philosophic error is arguably that he continually takes his bearings from the extreme or worst case ("*Ernstfall*"). The result of this tendency of thought is to conflate the reason for politics and the political with what is arguably only a necessary (not necessary and sufficient) condition for it to occur. The use of armed force in creating a protected space for the moderate reconciliation of differences through use of the political arts is clearly a necessary political condition, or pre-condition. Yet this is not to say that politics and the political are defined in an essential way by the definition of public enemies and by the decision for war.[4] Indeed, there are many conflicts in civilized life which require mediation, but which would never extend to war with-out it; and there are also extreme cases in life (e.g. floods, famines, plagues) which are not the product of war. Additionally, even conflicts which might eventually extend to the use of lethal force do not necessarily take their "meaning" from this extreme possibility — for civilized consciousness (and for Oakeshott in particular as we shall see)

Liberalism as not being serious implied that it denied (what Niehbur called) "the disorder introduced into the world by sin", and refused to confront it as a problem. Augustine had argued that wars would never end nor men beat their swords into ploughshares because war arose in the battle between the flesh and the spirit. Perhaps, for Schmitt, the Liberal vision of a commercially pacified world implied such an un-Augustinian project. Since Schmitt was writing his political-legal works in a secular context (he argued that current political concepts were secularized theological ones), perhaps he focused on resort to war as the extreme case, rather than on the sin which generated it. One never has the feeling with Schmitt that he has any particular interest or fascination with war and/or military culture — rather that (like Hobbes) he saw that it was the terrors of the belligerent state of nature in the mind's eye which could for a time transform the bourgeoisie into citizens. For a criticism from a Kantian standpoint of Schmitt's reliance upon the extreme or exceptional case, see Gerhardt (2003, pp. 205–218). It seems fitting that Kantian individualism should seem especially offended by Schmitt's arguments against Liberalism since, arguably, the centrality of duty and moral exertion in Kantian ethics makes it the species of Liberalism least susceptible to the charge of "not being serious".

4   Here is Hegel on this general point: "commonplace thinking often has the impression that force holds the state together, but in fact its only bond is the fundamental sense of order which everybody possesses" (1976, p. 282). Although in a notorious paragraph in this work Hegel praises war for its demographic effects, he is too rationalist and too bourgeois to accord war or death primary ontological status in the generation of the state.

they are what they are on their own terms at any given moment. Finally, political life is not just about reconciliation of differences; it is also about shared purposes, many of which are not remotely defined by avoidance or prosecution of war, any more than vast economic and engineering enterprises are defined by conquering or avoiding starvation. This point can be made clearer by contrasting Schmitt's account of the political with that of Aristotle, whose naturalism is not subject to the charge of ignoring the "real order of things".

Schmitt argues that "the political community transcends all other associations and societies" because of and "by virtue of this power over the physical life of man" (1976, p. 47). Aristotle, by contrast, argues in *The Politics* that the political community is sovereign over the other associations it comprehends, and that politics is the "master art" which prioritizes all the other arts to conform to some particular conception of justice.[5] By implication, Aristotle could be said to agree that if the decisions of the political community are not backed up by the credible threat of coercive measures, then the constitution or regime will not endure.[6] Yet while Aristotle could agree that "the political" is about some ruling others, for him its essence is not about managing enmity, but about making rules as good as possible for all concerned by saying how much of life is to be shared, or held in common. For Aristotle, political rule occurs among relative equals; is for the good of the ruled, not primarily the rulers; and often involves rotation of rulers. Aristotle does not make the logical error of defining any activity (including politics) in terms of the extreme case or the conditions without which it cannot occur, as does Schmitt, because, arguably, Aristotle is interested in the "fullness" of whatever he is depicting, not first and foremost with the practical or technical problems of how to preserve it under

---

[5]   Aristotle (1984, Book I). For the overstated view that between the thirteenth and sixteenth centuries the Greco-Roman vocabulary of politics as the art of good government was displaced by the vocabulary of reason of state, see Viroli (1992). The main problem with this argument is that Viroli conflates the views of Aristotle and Cicero (whose Latin had no word or concept for the Greek *politike*) into a single, "republican" paradigm, obscuring the fact that Aristotle has concepts and ideas for dealing with Machiavelli's idea of a good prince because politics for Aristotle involves people ruling people, whether in true or perverted regimes. Viroli is also silent on Augustinian Christianity's tarnishing of pagan political ideals long before the thirteenth century.

[6]   For Aristotle's observations on the relationship of constitutional development and military structure, see *Politics* (BK IV, Ch. 13). On this general subject the classic work is Delbrueck (1985).

any, including extreme, conditions, in the way that Machiavelli and Hobbes are, long in advance of Schmitt.[7]

II. Weber

A more subtle variation of the argument defining the political in terms of armed force is that of another twentieth-century German intellectual, Max Weber, the "founder" of modern sociology. Weber's fullest argument on the meaning of politics and the state occurs in a public lecture ("Politics as a Vocation") given in volatile domestic conditions just after Germany's surrender in the First World War. (Weber was also very concerned about the future of representative politics *vis-à-vis* the growth of "private" power in large-scale capitalism.[8]) In this lecture, Weber (without mentioning Kant) is concerned to encourage political responsibility by focusing his audience's attention on likely outcomes or results rather than merely good intentions, in assessing alternative courses of action. Of specific concern to us here is Weber's "sociological" definition of the state and politics. Weber begins by rejecting the view that the state (and politics) can be defined in terms of ends, for "there is scarcely any task some political association has not taken in hand", and there is no task that has been "exclusive and peculiar" to political associations or states (1946a, p. 77). We shall return to this claim in a moment, but for now let us see what Weber does with it.

Weber continues with the argument that since the state cannot be defined in terms of its ends, the "sociological" approach is to define it in terms of the specific means peculiar to it, namely "the use of physical force". Weber then defines the state as "a human community that (successfully) claims *the monopoly of the legitimate use of physical force* within a given territory" (*ibid.*, pp. 7–8).[9] And, although the state may delegate this right, it is "considered the sole source of the 'right' to use violence". Politics, for Weber, then becomes the activity of "striving to

---

7   Arguably, the logical development of Machiavelli's *Prince* and *Discourses* and Hobbes' *Leviathan* can be seen to flow from *avoidance* of an extreme condition — in the case of Machiavelli, fall from power or collapse of a regime, in the case of Hobbes, religious civil war. To see this point developed for Machiavelli, see Coats (2003, pp. 58–75).

8   For a recent, detailed description (with exhaustive English and German bibliography) of the intellectual and political context for both Weber's and Schmitt's writing, see Kelly (2003). Also useful in this regard are the lucid accounts of Weber and Schmitt in Thornhill (2000, pp. 18–91).

9   In German, this famous sentence reads: "Staat ist diejenige menschliche Gemeinschaft, welche innerhalb eines bestimmten Gebietes — dies: das 'Gebiet,' gehört zum Merkmal — das Monopol legitimer physicher Gewaltsamkeit für sich (mit Erfolg) beansprucht" (Weber, 1992, p. 6).

share power or striving to influence the distribution of power, either among states or among groups in a state" (1946a, pp. 7–8).[10] Let us examine this claim more closely.

To begin with, Weber's initial claim that states (and politics) cannot be identified in terms of ends (because so many have been claimed) is curious. The most obvious political end, and a defining one for many theorists and practitioners, has been the end or goal of achieving *justice*. This is Aristotle's claim, for instance, based on ancient Greek city-state practice and usage. The content of "justice" may vary from constitution to constitution, or from theorist to theorist (even Locke's defence of private property is in the name of justice), but it is a common and useful idea for defining the aim of a political association. It seems more likely that Weber rejects the idea of defining social entities in terms of ends because these involve "values" and thus would detract from the "scientific" character of Weber's "sociological" investigations, and not because definition in terms of ends lacks explanatory force.[11] So let us turn instead to Weber's treatment of political means on its own terms.

Weber's claim is that the only means peculiar to entities called states is the legitimate use of physical force (with politics understood as the activity of gaining power to influence or determine the policies of a state, including the "use of physical force"). Empirically and logically, this is a curious claim, since the "use of physical force" would seem a better fit for armies and police forces than political associations, which rely on a mixture of persuasion and coercive threat in exerting their control, reconciling differences, and deciding on common courses of action. In fact, if Weber were less reductionist in his analysis, he might have conceded that if one were going to focus on definition by means,

---

10   "'Politik' würde für uns also heissen: Streben nach Machtanteil oder nach Beeinflussung der Machtverteilung, sei es zwischen Staaten, sei es innerhalb eines Staates zwischen den Menschengruppen die er umschliesst" (Weber, 1992, p. 7).

11   For a defence of Aristotelian "social science" (*vis-à-vis* both modern social science and modern anthropological cultural relativism) for its comprehensiveness as well as its capacity to generate further inquiry, see Salkever (1991, pp. 11–12): "We find in them [The *Politics* and The *Ethics*] a discourse made up of arguable judgments of four major kinds: (1) descriptions of general facts or phenomena, the kind of thing that might be referred to as empirical assertions... (2) propositions about the efficient casual relationships of several phenomena or variables... (3) teleological propositions about the place of various activities in the lives of human beings, such as the claim that security and friendship are necessary, but not constitutive, conditions of political life; and finally (4) evaluative judgments both general and particular, such that political life is better than the life of war and conquest..."

the distinctive political means is arguably the *mixture* of both persuasive and coercive (i.e. their perceived, credible threat) measures in
deciding policy for an independent community or human grouping. As
in the case of Schmitt, Weber's approach to explaining the political is
partial and reductionist in taking its bearings from the solution to the
extreme case, without which it cannot exist, but which cannot thereby
be said to define it without making itself superfluous and redundant in
equating its function to that of an army or large police force.[12]

We might also observe in passing the similarities and differences
between Schmitt and Weber, on the one hand, and the philosopher of
war, von Clausewitz, on the other. In *On War*, von Clausewitz is not
concerned to explain politics as grounded in warfare, but to treat war
as rational in the sense of its being in service to political aims, as an
alternative to its being viewed as an autonomous activity of sheer
violence. In brief, one of his aims is to resist the tendency (in mass
warfare of the Napoleonic type) for the military aim (disarm the
enemy) to dominate what he calls the political aim. This means that von
Clausewitz must treat the use of armed force as a legitimate political
means under certain conditions, rather than as a cessation of political
interaction (as in the Grotian, Kantian, and Oakeshottian accounts):

> While policy (*Politik*) is apparently effaced in one kind of war (total) and
> yet is strongly evident in the other (limited), both kinds are equally
> political... *Only if politics is regarded as... cautious shying away from force*,
> could the second type of war (limited) appear to belong to politics more
> than the first (total). (von Clausewitz, 1976, p. 88)

III. Oakeshott

Let us turn now to Oakeshott's view of the relation between politics,
law, and the use of armed force in war, the exposition of which is
typically (for Oakeshott) treated in terms of opposition between two
Kantian-like ideal types, held in tension but never synthesized, and
which never treat political life as an unpurged residuum of the violence
and domination (*Herrschaft*) it is meant to abate or mitigate as in the
cases of Schmitt and Weber.

In his mature work, *On Human Conduct* (1975), Oakeshott draws
together and crystallizes themes on politics (and war) which he had

---

[12] For an interesting analysis of the relation between violence, coercion, and
economic and psychological deprivation, which concludes with the thought
that "coercion (or violence) should be treated as a class by itself... that
ought not to be lumped together... with material or social pressures", see
Etzioni (2007, pp. 102–103). For discussions of the various ways in which
war and violence undermine traditions and practices of politics, see Arendt
(1963, 1970). See also Gibbins (1986).

been working on for a lifetime, by way of identifying the characteristics and postulates of two ideal types of association implied in the theory and practice of European civilization over millennia—civil or moral association and enterprise association in pursuit of common, substantive wants. Politics here is identified as persuasive argument and activity about the desirability of terms of civil or moral association, and only metaphorically (1975, p. 162) attributed to persuasive argument directed toward the desirability of the terms (i.e. policies) of enterprise association ("metaphorically", since all of its terms are intended to facilitate substantive outcomes, a sub-political activity for Oakeshott).

I would like to suggest that Oakeshott's account of the difference between these two types of association can be conceived lucidly and without distortion as differences in the respective levels of *generality* at which they operate, and that this way of looking at them can also explain very well why Oakeshott argues that war, and preparation for war, are enemies to civil association, and, as well, to politics understood as debate over the desirability of its general terms.

In his essays from the 1950s Oakeshott refers to politics as the activity of "attending to the *general* arrangements of a society". This emphasis on *generality* is still a good point of departure for making more conceptually graspable Oakeshott's often fine distinctions about law and politics in *On Human Conduct*. In the latter work, Oakeshott is keen on the distinction between a general or moral purpose and a substantive or instrumental one as the basis for a clear distinction between civil association and enterprise association as pure, ideal types for analysis yet, in fact, the relationship between the two is a continuous one, starting in specific action and rising to generalities incapable of performance in single actions.

In the same fashion that Aristotle argues in the *Ethics* that action is always specific, Oakeshott (without actually defining it) is implying in his recurrent usage that the difference *between* a substantive purpose (e.g. getting in the harvest), and a general purpose (e.g. tranquility, happiness, civic virtue) is one of increasing generality. A substantive purpose can be unambiguously and visibly achieved in discrete actions, while a general, or moral, purpose can only be achieved in understanding and judgment concerning whether or not a series of discrete actions adequately subscribes to a generality or some general adverbial qualifications. In addition, Oakeshott's use of the term "instrumental purpose" appears to refer only to a specific, substantive purpose, not to a general purpose such as "civic virtue", apparently because there is no single action which could be unambiguously directed towards it. Carefully speaking then, and in spite his rhetorical denials, Oakeshott's civil or moral association can be "purposive" association, so long as its "purpose" is seen to be sufficiently general as to be incapable of specifying in advance any specific, substantive actions on the part of subscribers, and can only be achieved in acts of judgment subject to dispute by others.[13]

What, then, is the relationship *between* Oakeshott's account of war, and war preparation, *and* the politics of the ideal type, "civil association" (which has *some* overlap with existing states)? Oakeshott's concern about preparation for, prosecution of, and residual habits and institutions of, war is clearly that it reduces the politics of a civil association about the desirability of general societal arrangements to the "metaphorical" politics of enterprise association concerned with managing people and resources behind a single, overriding policy or purpose (victory in war). Since Oakeshott sees the states of modern Europe growing out of conditions of near continuous warfare (2006, pp. 373–386), he sees this vision of the basis of human association as very influential even in times of peace in providing the model for a "metaphorical" politics concerned primarily with choices over policies providing substantive benefits in return for requisite substantive actions. In brief, this vision has had the effect of purveying a near ubiquitous sense of the "equality of the besieged", thus endangering even the memory of an association of individual moral agents living and choosing under the latitude of general laws of association.

Oakeshott also rejects by implication the concept of "the political" as articulated by the ancient Greeks, the modern Germans, and contemporary writers such as Chantal Mouffe, preferring instead as a starting point the Roman republican idea of civil association among individuals subscribing to, or keeping faith with, general practices (the *mos maiorum*) in their individual actions. That is, the "political", seen as some sort of comprehensive context (whether "natural", organic, or historically created) for preserving the common good in the face of inescapable antagonisms, denies on Oakeshott's account the relationship of civility among individual agents who acknowledge and assent to general rules of just conduct. Oakeshott's account of politics (not "the political") is grounded on a Kantian-like postulate or assumption of individual moral agency and the "disciplined imagination" to discern the importance of recognizing the authority of rules as rules,

---

13   One could, of course, quibble that achievement of even a specific purpose such as getting in the harvest requires an act of judgment, but the point is that the problem of ambiguity becomes more acute as the purpose rises in generality. Also, achievement of a substantive purpose is *visibly* perceptible, whereas a general or moral purpose can only be achieved in an understanding, as in the difference between starting a fire (substantive and visual) and starting a fire as an arsonist (an understanding solely).

distinguished from their desirability and the substantive benefits contingently secured under them. Thus, we see that Oakeshott's critique of the concept of the "political" is constructed along the same lines as his critique of continuous war preparation—in its comprehensiveness of purpose and in its claim to be grounded in pre-reflective human nature it threatens to efface the possibility for practices of individual moral agency.

There is another aspect of Oakeshott's account of the relation between war and politics in the generation of the modern state which is worth inspecting for its relevance to contemporary world developments such as continuous conditions of insurgency and counter-insurgency. In his LSE lectures on the modern European state, Oakeshott observes, owing to the ubiquity in its history of war preparation, war fighting, and war conclusion, that formal declarations of war and conclusions of peace have become less significant in modern European politics *"as the distinction between war and peace has become more indefinite"* 14 (2006, p. 367). This development—the blurring of lines between war and peace—has profound implications for practices of politics, whether of civil or of enterprise association (where for the latter politics is simply deliberation and negotiation over policy). In both types, political discourse is still persuasive, not demonstrative nor authoritative discourse, and its possibility requires conditions of peace to provide the latitude for persuasion and negotiation over courses of action. If negotiation can now include (the threat and use of) bullets as well as words, then persuasive utterance, and with it politics, cannot long survive as a distinct and distinctive activity. (This is arguably why Kant insists that a state of peace must be *formally* instituted and grounded in political institutions and law.)

IV. Reflections: Oakeshott, Schmitt, Weber, von Clausewitz

I return now to my introductory claim that the respective expositional methods of our various theorists can go some way towards explaining their differences over the role of resort to use of armed force in both the definition and living practice of politics, because each respective method generates its own distinctive subject matter. More specifically,

---

14 Although Oakeshott does not discuss it, politics is not only becoming more like war, but war more like politics, as economists devise models for "pain infliction" as a means for achievement of political goals short of formal surrender. For a critique, see Coats (2009). For a discussion of the importance of formal institutions of peace in deterring the constant threat of force, see Nardin (1983, pp. 283–284).

we shall find that inspection of the presuppositions or postulates of each thinker's inquiry will illuminate their differences over the role of force in political life (or the political aspects of life, for Oakeshott).

Both Weber and Schmitt treat politics as simply a refinement or modification of a basic structure of power and domination (*Herrschaft*) inherent in human life together. Perhaps this orientation stems from a strategy to combat the "neutralization" of political life in the rise of capitalism and large state bureaucracies by reasserting the primitive aspects of life which become palpable in emergencies. Or perhaps they stem from a philosophic disposition to explain any phenomenon in terms of the extreme case ("*Ernstfall*") in order better to control it with certainty, as in the case of modern science, or in the strategies of Machiavelli and Hobbes for constitutional longevity; or even in the case of Heideggerian *Dasein* which is grounded in the certainty of death, rather than in the epiphenomenal "cogito sum".[15] At any rate, for a theorist such as Oakeshott, the expositional orientations of Schmitt, Weber, and von Clausewitz would all be instances of defining the legitimate role of coercion in ruling and policing a state as a residuum of the violence it is meant to abate, and hence as a logical confusion. Another way to state this criticism would be to say that their approach conflates a necessary precondition for the occurrence of politics (i.e. the use of armed force in sustaining spaces of moderation for the meaningful employment of persuasive utterance in the choice of political alternatives) with the activity of politics itself, and thereby risks "legitimizing" the threat and use of force as acceptable political means or tactics (*vs.* policing to deter criminal behaviour).

Oakeshott, by contrast, in *On Human Conduct* begins from an "ideal character" called "human conduct" and investigates (1) its postulates or presuppositions as well as (2) the past circumstances which nourished it by notionally converting a postulate of understanding into a moral ideal, thereby helping to make it discernible by the theorist, and (3) current circumstances which might eventually efface it as both a living practice and an ideal character to be investigated by the theorist. This ideal character of understanding requires the assumption of reflective, individual human consciousness in making contingent choices within a world of inherited practices and traditions. Oakeshott's concern with war preparation and war prosecution in his LSE lectures and in *On Human Conduct*, especially, is that over time a continual state of emergency requiring the mobilization of activity and resources behind an overriding purpose is incrementally eroding the "space" or latitude of individual citizens associated in terms of general, adverbial

---

15   See, in this connection, Heidegger (1985), Weber (1946a).

qualifications of conduct, as well as the disciplined imagination and delicacy to understand the difference *between* this kind of civil association *and* managerial association in terms of a few overriding specific purposes.

One might then contrast in the following way Oakeshott with the German theorists (excluding Kant!) on the relation of politics to use of armed force. Both Weber and Schmitt attempt to reassert the primacy of "the political" against the "neutralization" and technical and bureaucratic innovation of Liberalism and capitalism by viewing politics as a simply diluted form of *Herrschaft*, the most extreme forms of which will always dominate economic and bureaucratic forces. Oakeshott, by contrast, taking a much more historical view (including the idea that nature and human nature are merely learned, historic practices), is concerned to discern, identify, and specify a civilized achievement of modernity (i.e. practices of civility in politics and morals) before it is too late to remember them in the face of the growth and legacy of the managerial state. (In this endeavour Oakeshott is reminiscent of Hooker's sentiment in *The Laws of the Ecclesiastical Polity*, that "posterity may know we have not loosely through silence permitted things to pass away as in a dream".[16]) And, there is always the chance that by articulating anew for intellectual elites the individualist inheritance in European modernity, as well as its roots in Roman republican (*vs.* Greek) political culture, Oakeshott may help to give that *ethos* some renewed vitality.

On the question of the return to the Greek conception of the "political", it is illuminating to contrast Oakeshott, Weber, and Schmitt with Aristotle on the *polis*. Aristotle treats human beings as political beings because their highest natural faculty (capacity for reasoned speech — *logos*) can only be realized in the division of labour provided by *polis* association. For Aristotle, *polis* association and politics (the art of ordering a *polis*) are not diluted forms of domination and power, as with Weber and Schmitt, but the highest human form of creating order through use of rational and rhetorical arts of persuasion. While Aristotle concedes that who controls the use of arms in the *polis* controls the shape and longevity of the constitution, he never approaches any subject matter, including politics, solely in terms of efficient causality, as do the two German thinkers, although he does address that subject as well, including in his discussion of constitutional change in the fifth book of *Politics*, where much of the same advice on political longevity can be found as in Machiavelli's *Prince*. Rather, Aristotle's general approach is to depict the "fullness" of any subject matter he

---

16   Quoted in Voegelin (1952, title page).

approaches, eschewing by example the single-minded focus of the modern extreme case (*Ernstfall*) school of thought. Now, I want to suggest that in spite of their differences over nature and "the political" (Oakeshott strains[17] to include Aristotle in his discussion of human conduct), Oakeshott's approach shares with Aristotle a way of preserving the importance of persuasive utterance (*vs.* coercion) in his account of politics, including the "metaphorical" politics of enterprise association.

Oakeshott takes at face value the politics of civility as it appears in a strand of modern European cultural experience, without attempting to reduce it to a form of lordship or domination, since this would deny the possibility of a theoretical perspective or ideal character he calls human conduct, the only theoretical perspective capable of explaining human events without "explaining them away" in the fashion of reductionist "covering law" explanations, whether economic, psychological, organic, and so on. Yet by giving an account of politics from the perspective of human conduct (which presupposes individual moral agents capable of learning and choosing in response to self-understood contingencies), Oakeshott preserves the importance of politics as an activity of *persuasion* about better as against worse options for both constitutional shapes, as well as the policies pursued under them. In so doing, Oakeshott resists the tendency in modern theorists of "the political" to conflate as legitimate or acceptable political means the following: (1) the use of force; (2) the deterrent threat of force; and (3) persuasive arguments about "rational" courses of action for a body politic, since on their view politics is just diluted lordship. Oakeshott's warning voice here about the dangers of blurring the line between war and peace would seem especially relevant in a world where the Grotian system of strict demarcation between conditions of peace and war is under systemic attack. This attack comes from revolutionary strategies for endless insurgency (and hence endless counter-insurgent responses), strategies based on the view that the normal human condition is one of *bellum omnium contra omnes*, and that, by implication, swords, guns, and words are all acceptable negotiating tools; and that by implication, the Grotian and Westphalian system of using armed force defensively to create protected spaces (states) for moderation based on persuasion[18] was just a brief, passing phase in the history of the species.

---

17 See Oakeshott (1975, pp. 110 and 167).

18 For Oakeshott, the resort to war for the survival of the rule of law is compatible with civil association, which in such an emergency "circumstantially" transforms "the prescriptions of *lex* into a substantive purpose" (Oakeshott, 1975, p. 146). See, also, the discussion in Finn (2013, especially pp. 297–299). For older statements of the view that politics is just diluted

References

Arendt, H. (1970) *On Violence*, New York: Harcourt Brace.

Arendt, H. (1977) *On Revolution*, New York: Penguin Books.

Aristotle (1984) *The Politics*, Lord, C. (ed. & trans.), Chicago, IL: University of Chicago Press.

Coats, W.J. Jr. (2003) *Political Theory and Practice*, London: Associated University Presses.

Coats, W.J. Jr. (2009) *Armed Force and Moderate Political Life*, Lanham, MD: University Press of America.

Delbrueck, H. (1985) *History of the Art of War within the Framework of Political History*, 4 vols, Renfroe, W. (trans.), Westport, CT: Greenwood Press.

Etzioni, A. (2007) *Security First*, pp. 102–103, New Haven, CT: Yale University Press.

Finn, P. (2013) "The Challenges of War and Emergency to Nomocracy in Michael Oakeshott's Political Thought", in Henkel, M. & Lembcke, O. (eds.) *Praxis und Politik – Michael Oakeshott im Dialog*, pp. 283–300, Tübingen: Mohr Siebeck.

Gerhardt, V. (2003) "Politik als Ausnahme", in Mehring, R. (ed.) *Carl Schmitt: Der Begriff des Politischen*, pp. 205–218, Berlin: Academie Verlag.

Gibbins, J. (1986) "Violence and the Limits of Politics", paper presented at *ECPR Conference*, University of Gothenburg, Sweden, 7 April 1986.

Hegel, G.W.F. (1976) *Philosophy of Right*, Knox, T.M. (trans.), p. 282, Oxford: Oxford University Press.

Heidegger, M. (1985) *History of the Concept of Time*, Kisiel, T. (trans.), Bloomington, IN: Indiana University Press.

Hennis, W. (1988) *Max Weber: Essays in Reconstruction*, Tribe, K. (trans.), p. 249, London: Allen and Unwin.

Kelly, D. (2003) *The State of the Political*, pp. 159–160, 186, Oxford: Oxford University Press for the British Academy.

Meier, H. (2005) *Carl Schmitt and Leo Strauss: The Hidden Dialogue*, Lomax, J.H. (trans.), pp. 47–49, Chicago, IL: University of Chicago Press.

Nardin, T. (1983) *Law, Morality and the Relations of States*, pp. 283–284, Princeton, NJ: Princeton University Press.

Oakeshott, M.J. (1975) *On Human Conduct*, pp. 162, 272, Oxford: Clarendon Press.

Oakeshott, M.J. (2006) *Lectures in the History of Political Thought*, Nardin, T. & O'Sullivan, L. (eds.), pp. 367, 373–388, Exeter: Imprint Academic.

---

force and violence, see the classic Chinese Daoist work *Sun Tzu*; or see the characterizations of law by the Sophist, Thrasymachus, in the first book of Plato's *Republic*.

Salkever, S. (1991) "Aristotle's Social Science", in Lord, C. & O'Connor, D. (eds.) *Essays in the Foundations of Aristotelian Political Science*, pp. 11–12, Berkeley, CA: University of California Press.

Schmitt, C. (1976) *The Concept of the Political*, Schwab, G. (trans.), pp. 30, 34, 35, 47, New Brunswick, NJ: Rutgers University Press.

Strauss, L. (1976) "Comments on Carl Schmitt's *Der Bergiff des Politischen*", in Schmitt, C., *The Concept of the Political*, Schwab, G. (trans.), p. 99, New Brunswick, NJ: Rutgers University Press.

Thornhill, D. (2000) *Political Theory in Modern Germany*, pp. 18–91, Cambridge: Polity Press.

Voegelin, E. (1952) *The New Science of Politics*, Chicago, IL: University of Chicago Press.

von Clausewitz, C. (1976) *On War*, Howard, M. & Paret, P. (ed. & trans.), Princeton, NJ: Princeton University Press.

von Clausewitz, C. (1980) *Vom Kriege*, Troisdorf: Dümmler.

Viroli, M. (1992) *From Politics to Reason of State*, Cambridge: Cambridge University Press.

Weber, M. (1946a) "Politics as a Vocation", in Gerth, H. & Mills, C.W. (eds.) *From Max Weber*, p. 77, New York: Oxford University Press.

Weber, M. (1946b) "Religious Rejections of the World and their Directions", in Gerth, H. & Mills, C.W. (eds.) *From Max Weber*, pp. 323–359, New York: Oxford University Press.

Weber, M. (1992) *Politik als Beruf*, p. 6, Stuttgart: Reclam.

Concluding Postscript on the Continued Importance of Oakeshott and Foster

After a lifetime spent in academic and high public service and consulta-tion, 95-year-old Henry Kissinger has recently written a piece in a popular American intellectual magazine on the potential dangers to human culture and political life in fast evolving artificial intelligence or "AI" ("How the Enlightenment Ends"[1]). In it, Kissinger calls on special-ists in AI to join him in exploring concerns over its effects on human civilization. Among these concerns: whereas the automation of the industrial age was concerned with the *means* to humanly contrived *ends*, self-learning AI is concerned with *ends* which it arrives at *not* through *contextual* thinking, but through highly accelerated experi-mentation involving millions of cases to correct or "tweek" its own algorithms.

Another way to say this (not Kissinger's) is that AI doesn't need a realm for general context and judgment from universals to particulars, because it produces specialized results for particular problems at the speed of light, so to speak; and this is what the general population wants from it, slowly changing its own way of thinking and lessening its capacity for judgment within general contexts.

Arguably, the political and economic freedom achieved for large numbers of people in liberal democracies (and constitutional monarchies) of the past three centuries has come in an intermediate realm of institutionalized individual judgment and choice in parlia-ments and markets, arguably an outcome prefigured in Aristotle's insight that politics (and the mixed regime) were achievements of

---

1   Kissinger, H. (2018) "How the Enlightenment Ends", *The Atlantic*, pp. 11–14.

middling[2] kinds of people.[3] Arguably, the insights secured and articulated by Oakeshott and Foster about the differences between creativity
and craft as approaches to human self-understanding, and the advantages of the former for cultivation of individual freedom, when widely
understood (often in a religious idiom), provide a bulwark against the
incremental elimination by "AI" of a realm of middling human judgment in the organization of life. And, arguably again, it provides a
better bulwark than reliance on the *techne* model of human organization favoured by Plato and Confucius, which can easily employ "AI"
and "IT" to reduce populations to the analogue of inert material (such
as a potter's clay) waiting to be formed — a project already underway in
the world's most populous country.

In a completely AI-ordered world, the contingent realm of human
freedom subsisting in the judgmental gap between *general* aims and
specific actions and policies would become superfluous, unnecessary,
and meaningless. In Oakeshottian terms, the capacity to distinguish
between civil and enterprise association would slowly fade. The
appearance of AI has made clear that "putting things in context" was a
distinctively human kind of "short-hand" no longer necessary for
cooperative projects, when billions of particular cases can be sorted by
super computers in the twinkling of an eye. Preserving a realm of
contextual judgment in an "AI world" will require awareness, foresight, and contrivance.

---

2   That is, those *independent* enough not to be satisfied living under a despot,
     but *dependent* enough on one another to need a cooperative language and
     practice — the vocabulary and practice of politics, distinguished from more
     specific logistical and military vocabularies and practices.
3   For development of this theme, see Leslie G. Rubin (2018) *America, Aristotle
     and the Politics of a Middle Class*, Waco, TX: Baylor University Press.

Modern Political Effects of Medieval Creation–Eternity Debates

This talk argues that medieval debates in the writings of especially Moses Maimonides and Thomas Aquinas concerning the creation versus eternity of the universe ("the All") had an important, subsequent effect on European conceptions of political order. In brief, the paper speculates that by giving the theory of creation *ex nihilo* a philosophic respectability (though holding it indemonstrable) lacking since Parmenides' quip that "out of nothing, nothing comes", these debates made conceivable and possible a "creative" alternative to the political *techne* model for generating political order expounded in Plato's *Republic*.

The talk will proceed by exploring the implications for its theme in *The Guide of the Perplexed* by Moses Maimonides, who arguably shows a clearer apprehension than Thomas Aquinas's often obfuscatory account in the *Summa Theologica*, of the profound philosophic and practical implications flowing from the biblical account of a created (*vs.* an eternal) universe. (And, this, regardless of where Maimonides' own sympathies may have been in this debate.) It faithfully attempts to summarize Maimonides' argument in Part III, Chapter 13, and then draw upon this summary to articulate the differences between a crafted *and* a created object (including a human being). Finally, it will speculate briefly on how the idea of creation influenced conceptions of the origins of political order in modern thinkers such as Hobbes and Rousseau.

In his twelfth-century, Arabic language masterpiece the Jewish thinker Maimonides ostensibly writes to a former disciple perplexed by apparent differences *between* biblical revelation and law *and* the Greek philosophical inheritance alive in southern Spain for several centuries among the three Abrahamic faiths. In Part II, Chapters 13–25,

Maimonides lays out the various differences *between* especially Plato and Aristotle *and* the biblical account of creation, indicating his reasons for preferring the latter, and then in Part III, Chapter 13, he shows in some detail how the theory of creation differs from a teleological account of both the world and human beings. It is this latter subject I wish to explore in order to highlight the differences between a created and an eternal, teleological world and universe.

In Part III, Chapter 13, Maimonides begins by observing that purpose adheres only to that which has passed from non-existence into existence through the action of an external agent, and since God is eternal, it is meaningless to ask the purpose or final cause of his existence. After a digression on Aristotle (who "holds the eternity of the universe"), Maimonides turns to the view of those supporters of the theory of creation out of nothing that "all that has been made exists only for the human species so that it should worship God" (1963, p. 451). He proceeds to critique this view through the stages of a *reductio ad absurdum* to arrive at the "correct answer", which is that all that can be said of the purpose of creation is that it was the Will of God:

> Thus… the quest for the final end of all… collapses. For we say that in virtue of His will He has brought into existence all the parts of the world, some of which have been intended for their own sakes, whereas others for the sake of some other thing that is intended for its own sake. (*ibid.*, p. 452)

And God has created all, of himself, and for his own glory, "and for no other purpose". Even objects of creation, such as stars and human beings, are not ascribed a purpose carefully speaking, says Maimonides, but only given a specific nature, such as the ability to give light or have dominion over the fish of the sea, respectively. Maimonides concludes this discussion by observing again that we "are obliged to believe that all that exists was intended… according to His volition". And, again, "we shall seek no other cause or final end" whatever, except for "His volition" (*ibid.*, p. 454).

Now, what are the implications of Maimonides' characterizations of the theory of creation *ex nihilo* and how might they be summarized? Before turning to this question, it will be useful to look briefly at another piece of Maimonides' text, concerning various theories of the genesis or eternity of the universe ("the All"). In Part II, Ch. 13 of *The Guide*, Maimonides distinguishes "our" theory of creation out of nothing from the Platonic theory, the Aristotelian theory, and the godless theory of the Epicureans. The relevant point here is the care Maimonides takes to correct the imprecise view "among us" that Plato's account in *The Timaeus* of a divine craftsman is of "the same belief that we have". His point is that the Platonic theory assumes the pre-existence of some primary substance which the divine Craftsman subsequently informs or shapes, while "we believe that the heaven was generated out of nothing after a state of absolute non-existence…" And, again, Maimonides concludes that "every follower of the Law of Moses and Abraham… is to believe that there is nothing eternal in any way… with God"; and that "the bringing into existence out of non-existence is for the deity not an impossibility…" (1963, pp. 284–285).

Now, let us attempt to gather up the relevant implications for our theme of Maimonides' discussion of the difference between a created and an eternal universe. On Maimonides' interpretation of the biblical account of creation, God wilfully created "the All" (to include form, matter, and time) for no purpose other than the act of creation itself and "for Himself". No final, pre-existing cause can be identified, and even God's creations such as stars and human beings are not ascribed purposes on this account, carefully speaking, but rather only certain characteristics. Nor can a comprehensive, ascending chain of teleological purposes be presumed in a created universe (the view of Thomas Aquinas to the contrary notwithstanding).

Implied elements of this account might be described in more modern philosophic language as the ideas that *contingency* is essential to nature and *will* to both God and human beings. Additionally, although we did not inspect Maimonides on Mosaic law (III, Chs. 31, 33), he says that while the law has both rational and moral benefits, the obligation to obey derives not from its wisdom or morality, but from its being the expression of wilful, divine *commandment*. In more modern terminology we might render the implication of this insight by saying that *positivity* is essential to law, though its rationality and morality are not thereby excluded.

Now, how might we contrast this account of a wilfully created universe "from nothing" with the teleological, ontologically-dualist account of the Greek rationalist philosophers, especially as given and implied in *The Republic* of Plato? What follows is a condensed, interpretive account which hopefully is not controversial in its mere characterizations.

As in generally known, on the Greek Rationalist worldview, both form and matter are given eternally; the essence of any object is its "detachable" form which is known by intellection; matter adds nothing positive to form; and both thinking and making are purposive and involve discovering and copying pre-existing forms or models. Even Plato's divine craftsman in *The Timaeus* only moulds or informs pre-existing matter into pre-existing forms.

By contrast, the account of cosmological "creation" in the ancient Hebrew and early Christian texts entails the ideas that creation is not purposive in the Greek sense, that is, it is not directed toward a distinctively conceived and antecedently existing end or form in advance of the act of wilful creation; and, by implication, in creation, and in a created (versus crafted object) there is no intellectively graspable form distinguished from its accidental embodiment.

Several more implications follow. Creation is an act of will which can exceed regulations prescribed by reason. Contingency is an important aspect of created objects (including physical nature and human beings), that is, their "accidental" embodiments are not necessitated by, nor can be deduced from, their form or idea. And, finally, there can be no degrees of being in creation as there are in the Greek concept of *ousia*: if something is created *ex nihilo*, "it must be entirely present as soon as it has ceased to be wholly absent" (Foster, 1934, p. 464, note 1). (Hence the impossibility of an ascending chain of more perfect ends in a created universe; in such a universe, so-called "lower" beings are no less *real* than "higher" ones, an insight about the reality of matter which eventually makes possible modern empirical science.)

It is instructive at this point, by way of further illumination of the difference between a created and crafted object, to consider the case of modern political sovereignty contrasted with the case of the political craftsman in Plato's *Republic*. The idea of the state (*vs.* the *polis*), as articulated especially by Hobbes and Rousseau, requires the presence of a sovereign will which creates or imposes upon itself its own constitutional form (a creative act definitionally), contrasted with Plato's account of a founder as constitutional craftsman, standing outside the *polis* and forming or in-forming an inert, citizen subject matter. The modern state, by contrast, is created or "artificial" (as men imitate God's art in Hobbes' usage) because (1) it is the product of a sovereign will which informs itself (clearer in Rousseau than Hobbes); (2) it is informed by no antecedently existing and conceptually distinct purpose (Hobbes omits final causality in the *Leviathan's* subtitle); and (3) therefore its essence cannot be separated from its existence by philosophic intellect and used as an external standard against which to critique existing states, which, by implication, can only be judged historically. Additionally, since the modern state's existence cannot be separated from its essence, its realization (as in the case of Anselm's ontological proof for the existence of God) inheres in it, or completes it in a way that Plato has Socrates explicitly deny to the ideal *polis* of *The Republic* in the conclusion to Book IX where Socrates is explicitly indifferent to the actualization of the *callipolis*, except as a model for internal order in the souls of certain rare individuals.

By way of summary of my argument, I'll simply note that this paper is predicated upon the observation that Western civilization of the past five centuries or so ("modernity") is (1) characterized by the increasing tension with, and even liberation from, Greek intellectual forms, modern Enlightenment rationalism to the contrary notwithstanding; (2) that this liberation has been led by the largely implicit spread of the idea of "creativity" in both thought and action, as initially developed in medieval creation–eternity debates; and (3) that the idea of the "creative" provides a speculative basis for appreciation of the concomitant spread of diversity and plurality, with all of its attendant cultural *advantages* and political-constitutional disadvantages.[1] (That is, if the creative deconstruction of all inherited hierarchy issues in the validation of all difference, then some sort of crisis of authority would seem inevitable, and, in fact, is already underway.)

Finally, in terms of the conference theme, the role of medieval texts in illuminating the origins of the spread of "creativity" in thought and action is almost too obvious to state for the constitutive elements of modern and post-modern secular identity. In a longer talk this progression could be traced from the fourteenth-century British voluntarist/nominalist thinker William of Ockham's theories about the freedom of both divine and human will (and the role of government as a mere external check upon human freedom) to Germany where he emigrated, and where it eventually appears in its purest form in the Kantian account of the autonomy of the human, moral will.

References

Dupré, L. (1993) *Passage to Modernity*, p. 249, New Haven, CT: Yale University Press.

Foster, M.B. (1934) "The Christian Doctrine of Creation and the Rise of Modern Natural Science", *Mind*, Vol. 43, p. 464.

Maimonides, M. (1963) *The Guide of the Perplexed*, Pines, S. (trans.), Chicago, IL: University of Chicago Press.

Strauss L. (1952) "On Collingwood's Philosophy of History", *Review of Metaphysics*, Vol. 5, 4, pp. 572–573.

---

[1] For a critical view of the effects of "the creative" for conflating knowing with doing and making, see Leo Strauss's long review of R.G. Collingwood, *The Idea of History* (1952), especially pp. 572–573. For a more positive view of "the creative" see Foster (1934). For the view that modernity is characterized by less, not more, diversity, see Dupré (1993, p. 249).

Index